WHAT TO USE INSTEAD

A Handbook
of Practical Substitutes

WHAT TO USE
INSTEAD

Carol Ann Rinzler

PHAROS BOOKS
A SCRIPPS HOWARD COMPANY
NEW YORK

Cover and text design by Nancy Eato
Illustrations by Carlos Torres

First published in 1987.

Distributed in the United States by Ballantine Books, a division
of Random House, Inc., and in Canada by Random House of
Canada, Ltd.

Library of Congress Cataloging-in-Publication Data

Rinzler, Carol Ann.
What to use instead.

Bibliography: p.186
Includes index.
1. Substitute products.   2. Food substitutes.
3. Household supplies.   I. Title.
TX147-R5   1987   640   87-60158
ISBN 0-88687-322-3 (Pharos Books)
ISBN 0-345-34879-6 (Ballantine Books)

Printed in the United States of America.

Pharos Books
A Scripps Howard Company
200 Park Avenue
New York, NY 10166

10 9 8 7 6 5 4 3 2 1

■

*This book is dedicated to my friend,
Adam Matthew Goldberg, to celebrate
his special day, October 17, 1987.*

■

CONTENTS

■

SEASONINGS

■

PREFACE

Your nose is running, your throat is sore and everything aches. What you need is a cup of hot tea, with honey and lemon. You've got the tea and the honey, but the lemon is a shriveled yellow ball past its prime. So you toss out the lemon and use a drop or two of _____ instead.

Or your idea of bliss is a steaming hot tub full of soothing bath salts, but if your tastes are rich, your budget isn't. So you keep the budget balanced by steering past pricey bath salts to the old-fashioned (but satisfyingly effective) _____ instead.

Or your recipe for onion dip calls for sour cream. You'd like to cut down on the calories, fat and cholesterol by using yogurt, but your family loathes the taste. You cleverly solve the problem by using _____ instead.

Or, you're sensitive to the soap in all the well-known brands of scouring pads. Sometimes you can get by with plastic scrubbing pads, but for really heavy-duty work, you use _____ instead.

If you've already been through this set of situations, you may know that you can fill in the blanks with *plain white vinegar* instead of lemon juice; *baking soda* instead of bath salts; *very well drained yogurt* (draining smoothes the taste and thickens the texture) instead of sour cream; and *fine steel wool,* either plain or saturated with your regular dishwashing liquid.

These are only a few examples of how a handy, available substitute from your own kitchen, bathroom, or laundry cabinet can fill in for an exotic ingredient or one you've forgotten to buy.

Many of the alternatives listed in this book were born of a desperate need to find something (anything!) that would work when I was out of something. Moments like that tend to encourage your imagination.

And let's not forget the household budget. Do you really need a special cleaner for every kind of metal in the house or a different detergent for every load of wash? Of course not. The alternatives listed here will tell you what to use economically instead.

Before you start thumbing your way through this book, let's face one thing squarely. Useful though they may be, some of my alternatives (particularly those for food and wine) are guaranteed to raise the hackles of purists who believe that only the real thing works. Well, the real thing may be nice (who wouldn't prefer whipped cream to a substitute made with dried milk powder or evaporated milk?) but it isn't always around when you need it. Or safe. Or good for you. Life, alas, is far from perfect and occasionally compromise is the only way to go.

Since every cook and housekeeper has his or her own personal bag of tricks that make the job faster and easier, there's room for you to list your own favorites at the end of each section, under the heading, "Notes: Your own alternatives."

Carol Ann Rinzler
June 1987

NOTE TO THE READER

If you are sensitive to any food or chemical ingredient or have experienced an allergic reaction after using one; if you have a medical condition that necessitates a special diet; or if you are using medication prescribed by your doctor, *always* check with your doctor before using *any* alternatives or substitutes, including those listed here. Your own doctor, the person most familiar with your medical history, is your best guide to the safe use of food, cosmetics, and health care and household products.

Some of the product brand names in this book are registered trademarks.

PERSONAL CARE

BABY CARE

As a new parent,
you'll probably head
straight for the baby section
in your drugstore.
But does your infant
really need all those
special creams and lotions?
Can you and your baby
share the same shampoo?
Can you warm a baby bottle
without a baby-bottle warmer?
No. Yes. Maybe. Of course.

■ ■   BABY CREAM AND LOTION   ■ ■

WHAT TO USE INSTEAD

Regular skin creams and lotions.   There is no special formula for a baby lotion, although products for babies generally do not contain coloring agents or heavy perfumes. Compare the ingredient list on a regular product such as Vaseline Intensive Care Lotion with the label on your favorite baby lotion, and you'll find that *all* skin creams contain wax (beeswax, ceresin, paraffin), oil (mineral oil, petroleum jelly), and water. Lotions do too, but they have proportionally more water than creams, which is why they are liquid, not solid, and why they evaporate and dry more quickly on your skin.

■ ■   BABY OIL   ■ ■

WHAT TO USE INSTEAD

Mineral oil.   That's what you'll find in baby oil, some of which also contain a fragrance. If you're willing to do without the fragrance, you should be able to save money by using plain mineral oil instead.

Petroleum jelly (such as Vaseline).   Petroleum jelly is hardened mineral oil. A superb protector, it coats the skin effectively, keeping natural moisture in. It may also be useful in some cases of diaper rash caused by irritating wetness against the baby's bottom; a protective layer of petroleum jelly may keep the wetness from touching the baby's skin.

■ ■   BABY POWDER   ■ ■

WHAT TO USE INSTEAD

Cornstarch.   It's cheap and pure (no perfumes, no colors).

It's also impressively absorbent: cornstarch can absorb up to twenty-five times as much moisture as ordinary talcum powder can.

Regular bath powder.   You and your baby can share any bath powder that has no antiseptics or fungicides. (Medicated powders should be used only on the advice of a physician. That goes for you *and* your baby.)

DO NOT use boric acid. Boric acid is a systemic poison that can be absorbed through skin and mucous membranes. It is not a safe alternative to baby powders.

■■   BABY SHAMPOO   ■■

WHAT TO USE INSTEAD

Any mild shampoo that contains no antidandruff ingredients, chemicals to color or "color-correct" your hair, or conditioners (they make adult hair manageable but can turn a baby's fine hair sticky). Some baby shampoos contain formaldehyde, an extremely effective mold inhibitor that keeps the shampoo safe from fungi. Unfortunately, formaldehyde is also an irritant, an allergen, and a potent allergic sensitizer that may make a baby or an adult sensitive to other ingredients. When you're looking for substitutes, it's not a bad idea to look for a shampoo without formaldehyde.

Bath soap.   In a pinch you can wash your baby's hair with bar soap, but that soap is not formulated to dissolve as efficiently as shampoo. If you use it frequently instead of shampoo, it will leave a sticky scum on your baby's hair.

■■   BOTTLE WARMER   ■■

WHAT TO USE INSTEAD

Hot running water.   Take the bottle out of the refrigerator and hold it under the running water for a minute or two until it feels pleasantly warm to the touch.

■ ■   **TEETHING LOTION**   ■ ■

WHAT TO USE INSTEAD

Teething ring, or a hard sweetened biscuit (rusk).   Teething lotions contain local anesthetics (usually benzocaine), that numb the gum and relieve the pain of teething. Chewing on hard objects such as a teething ring or a hard sweet rusk biscuit may also relieve the discomfort. If your baby is still uncomfortable, check with your doctor, who may prescribe aspirin or another analgesic for longer, more effective relief.

NOTES: YOUR OWN ALTERNATIVES

_____

_____

_____

_____

_____

_____

_____

_____

_____

_____

FOR THE BATH

The human soul craves
a warm and soothing bath.
Cleopatra soaked in milk.
Roman senators
debated in public pools.
Proper Victorians
"took the waters"
at Bath and Baden-Baden.
At home, you can pamper
mind and body with homemade
alternatives to pricey
bath oils and salts.

■■   ANTIPERSPIRANT   ■■

WHAT TO USE INSTEAD

Cornstarch.   Antiperspirant sprays and liquids contain astringents such as aluminum salts that make the skin swell slightly and slow the production of moisture. Cornstarch, which is strictly a last-ditch, there's-nothing-else-available alternative, won't slow down the production of moisture, but it *is* a super absorbent.

CAUTION: Don't rely on cornstarch to protect a delicate dress, blouse, or sweater. In fact, if you perspire heavily, even a commercial antiperspirant may not protect the clothes. The only guaranteed protection is dress shields.

■■   BATH OIL   ■■

WHAT TO USE INSTEAD

Mineral oil.   Add a tablespoon oil to a warm bath, and be *very* careful getting in and out of the tub. All bath oils make the surface of the bathtub extremely slippery.

DO NOT use baby oil. Baby oils usually contain fragrances; they may be irritating to sensitive body tissues.

■■   BATH SALTS   ■■

WHAT TO USE INSTEAD

Baking soda (sodium bicarbonate).   Add 2 or 3 tablespoons to a tub of warm water for a satisfying soak. But don't use any bath salts, even bicarbonate of soda, if your skin is dry. All bath salts will make your skin dryer.

DO NOT use baking powder. Baking powder is sodium bicarbonate mixed with cream of tartar, a thickener and anti-caking ingredient.

■■ **BUBBLE BATH** ■■

WHAT TO USE INSTEAD

Bar soap. Hold the soap under a fast-running faucet to fill the tub with bubbles. This alternative is less irritating than bubble baths, which have often been implicated in urinary infections. It's also cheaper. A bar of Ivory soap is particularly good for making bubbles. (They don't last long, but there are lots of them.)

DO NOT use shampoo, dishwashing liquids, laundry soap, or detergent powder. Shampoos contain preservatives, colors, and fragrances in concentrations considered safe for use on a small area (your scalp) but not all over your body. Dishwashing liquids and laundry products contain strong detergents, brighteners, bleaches, and water softeners that can irritate skin as well as mucous membranes. Skip them all.

■■ **DEODORANT** ■■

WHAT TO USE INSTEAD

Baking soda (sodium bicarbonate). The good news is that baking soda absorbs and dissipates odors. The bad news is that it's not an antiperspirant. Consider this a last-ditch substitute or a substitute for someone who's sensitive to all the commercial products, including the hypoallergenic ones.

■■   DUSTING POWDER   ■■

WHAT TO USE INSTEAD

Cornstarch.   Most dusting powders for the bath are made primarily of talc, which is why they are called talcum powders. Some, such as Johnson's Baby Powder, are simply talc plus fragrance; others may contain rice starch, wheat starch, or cornstarch as fillers plus preservatives and anticaking agents such as calcium or magnesium carbonate, kaolin, or zinc stearate to keep the powder pouring freely. "Medicated" powders contain an antiseptic or fungicide. Cornstarch is a cheap, handy, additive-free alternative that can absorb up to 25 times as much moisture as talc can.

NOTES: YOUR OWN ALTERNATIVES

_____

_____

_____

_____

_____

_____

_____

_____

_____

_____

_____

_____

_____

_____

_____

_____

_____

_____

_____

_____

_____

_____

_____

_____

_____

_____

_____

_____

_____

_____

_____

_____

_____

COSMETICS

Strictly speaking,
a cosmetic is anything you rub,
spill, or spray on your skin
to make you cleaner or better-looking.
If it promises a medical benefit,
it's not a cosmetic.
What we're talking about here
is makeup, the products
whose only function
is to make you look great.

■■   BLUSHER (ROUGE)   ■■

WHAT TO USE INSTEAD

Lipstick.   Draw a line on your cheek and blend it in with some foundation makeup or a little hand lotion.

You can't reverse this substitution and use your blusher or rouge as lipstick, since they may contain colors and other ingredients not permitted in cosmetics or drugs meant to be swallowed or that, like lipstick, may be swallowed accidentally.

■■   CONTOURING POWDER   ■■

WHAT TO USE INSTEAD

Soft brown eyebrow pencil.   Stroke on the color and blend it in with foundation liquid.

You can use eye cosmetics on your cheek but you can't use brown contouring powder as eyeshadow unless the label specifically says you can. Cosmetics meant to be used on the cheeks may contain colors or other additives not permitted in cosmetics meant to be used around the eyes.

■■   FACE POWDER   ■■

WHAT TO USE INSTEAD

Cornstarch.   It's cheap, available, and additive-free; a dab will take the shine off your nose. But use the cornstarch with care: a dab too much, and you'll look ghostly.

■ ■   FACIAL MASQUE   ■ ■

WHAT TO USE INSTEAD

Egg white, whipped or straight from the shell.   As the proteins in the egg white dry, they may pull dirt and debris to the surface of your skin or loosen the dead cells that slough off the top layer of your skin naturally every day. Wash off the dry egg white and your skin may temporarily look smoother and fresher.

A soft, dry washcloth.   Rub the cloth gently over your face to brush away the dead cells on top of your skin.

■ ■   FOUNDATION MAKEUP   ■ ■

WHAT TO USE INSTEAD

Face powder plus hand lotion.   Blend two parts tinted face powder with one part hand lotion and apply to face.

ALWAYS DISCARD THE LEFTOVERS. The mixture can't be stored, both because it will separate and because it doesn't have the preservatives necessary to protect it from microbial contamination.

■ ■   LIP GLOSS   ■ ■

WHAT TO USE INSTEAD

Mineral oil.   This oil is the active ingredient in all commercial lip glosses.

Petroleum jelly (Vaseline).   This is stickier and harder to use than mineral oil but if you're careful it might work.

■■ **MAKEUP BRUSHES** ■■

WHAT TO USE INSTEAD

Paint brushes. When sable-bristle makeup brushes may cost more than $50, the equally soft and bushy watercolor brushes at your local hardware or art-supply store are a stunning bargain for applying blush and face powder. Of course, you only use *new,* clean brushes, *never* ones that have been cleaned after being used to paint something.

Cotton swabs (Q-tips). Cotton swabs are useful as a cheap and handy alternative to eyeshadow applicators. They have the additional benefit of being disposable, which means that if you brush them against the eyeshadow, then apply the shadow to your lids and immediately discard the swab, you don't have to worry about contaminating the shadow with the bacteria that live naturally on your skin—a definite plus for cosmetics or applicators used around the eyes.

■■ **NAIL POLISH (CLEAR)** ■■

WHAT TO USE INSTEAD

Petroleum jelly. For a fast shine without polish, rub petroleum jelly onto a clean, polish-free nail, then buff with a clean, soft, lint-free towel until the nail shines.

■■ **NAIL POLISH REMOVER** ■■

WHAT TO USE INSTEAD

Nail polish. When you're out of remover or have to repair a chipped nail in a hurry, paint the nail with a fresh coat of polish and quickly wipe it off to remove the layer of old polish underneath, leaving a smooth surface you can repaint without chips. It works because nail polish, like nail polish remover, contains solvents (acetone or amyl acetate) that dissolve polish. The solvents keep the polish from drying out in the bottle.

■■ NAIL PATCH ■■

WHAT TO USE INSTEAD

Facial tissue or the silicone-coated paper used to clean eye glasses. Start with your nails (or one damaged nail) stripped of polish. Cut out a small piece of paper or tissue, either a strip to lay across a break or a patch to cover the whole nail. Paint the nail with a fresh coat of colorless polish. Immediately lay the piece of paper flat on the wet nail and push or pull it into place with a tweezer. If necessary, fold it over the tip of the nail and tuck it under. As soon as the paper is in place, flat on the nail, paint it with a second coat of colorless polish. Let the patch dry, then manicure as usual. This procedure takes a lot of practice and it's not as effective as professional patching, but it may hold a broken or split nail in place until you can get expert attention.

■■ PERFUME ■■

WHAT TO USE INSTEAD

Toilet water, cologne, aftershave. These are all less pricey alternatives to perfume. What makes them less expensive? They contain more water and alcohol, less of the actual aromatic ingredient.

NOTES: YOUR OWN ALTERNATIVES

_____

_____

_____

_____

_____

_____

_____

_____

_____

_____

_____

_____

_____

_____

_____

_____

_____

_____

_____

_____

HAIR CARE

Eggs, oils, herbs, and fruit—
if it's good to eat,
chances are
its good for your hair.
But the kitchen
isn't the only place
to look for alternatives
to commercial conditioners,
rinses, and shampoos.
Many commercial products
can also be used
in several ways, saving pennies
as they clean and
shine your hair.

■■ COLOR RINSE ■■

WHAT TO USE INSTEAD

Camomile tea. Steep one camomile teabag in a cup of hot water until the water is golden. Then dilute the cup of strong camomile tea with three cups of lukewarm water and pour the camomile water through your hair. It will put golden highlights into light hair.

DO NOT use this rinse if you are sensitive to ragweed, marigolds, or asters. Camomile, which belongs to the same plant family, may trigger allergic reactions in sensitive individuals. In fact, if you are sensitive to *any* plants, it is always best to check with your doctor before using "natural" alternatives made from plants.

Laundry bluing. One teaspoon bluing in 11 ounces warm water will give a blue cast to gray or white hair.

Orange pekoe tea or sage tea. Steep a teabag in a cup of boiling water for three minutes (or until the water is a pleasant shade of amber). Then let the water cool. When it is lukewarm, pour it through your hair. Leave the solution on your hair for about half an hour, and then rinse thoroughly with clear water. This rinse darkens the hair.

■■ CONDITIONING RINSE ■■

WHAT TO USE INSTEAD

Lemon juice, vinegar, cool tea. Shampoos are alkaline; they may leave a dulling, sticky mineral residue on your hair and cause the keratin (protein) in the hair to swell. An acid rinse such as water combined with lemon juice, vinegar, or cool tea can dissolve the sticky residue and reduce the swelling of the keratin, making your hair shinier and more manageable ("conditioning" it). Use the lemon on blond hair and the cool tea on dark hair; vinegar will work on either one.

■■ CREAM CONDITIONER ■■

WHAT TO USE INSTEAD

Olive oil, mayonnaise. Coat your hair with oil or mayonnaise, wrap your head in a thick towel or cover it with plastic wrap, let the whole thing sit for half an hour, and then shampoo. When your hair dries, it should be smoother and look shinier.

CAUTION: If you use mayonnaise, take the simple but important precaution of scooping it out of the jar with a clean spoon, not your fingers, to avoid contaminating the remaining mayonnaise.

Eggs. The oily yolk of a fresh egg adds shine; the protein in the egg white adds body. Rub the egg into your hair and let it sit there for a while before shampooing or mix it with a half-cup of shampoo and wash your hair as usual. Either way, be sure to rinse thoroughly.

■■ DRY SHAMPOO ■■

WHAT TO USE INSTEAD

Cornstarch. Cornstarch is the active ingredient in dry shampoos. Spread it gently through your hair, wait a few minutes while it absorbs oils and dirt, then brush thoroughly to remove the powder. The cornstarch is not as efficient as a regular, wet shampoo, but it will remove some of the dirt and oil on your hair when you don't have time to shampoo.

■■   HAIR LIGHTENER   ■■

WHAT TO USE INSTEAD

Lemon juice.   Yes, this old-fashioned standby will lighten your hair slightly if you sit in the sun for a while after rinsing or streaking it through your hair.

■■   HAIR SPRAY   ■■

WHAT TO USE INSTEAD

Hair-styling mousse.   After your hair has dried and been styled, squirt about a tablespoon of mousse foam into your palm, rub your palms gently together to spread the mousse and smooth your palms over your hair to leave a thin glaze of mousse, to hold your hair in place. An extra bonus: The mousse makes your hair shinier and thicker.

■■   HAIR-STYLING MOUSSE   ■■

WHAT TO USE INSTEAD

Beer or champagne.   As the liquid evaporates, the sugars in the beverage will dry to form a stiff film that helps hold your hair in place.

DO NOT use a dark beer on light hair (you'll darken the hair color) and don't use either beer or champagne if your hair is very dry since the alcohol will make it even drier.

Hair spray.   Spray your hair while it's still wet, then set your hair or simply let it dry. The spray contains resins that form a stiff film to hold your hair in place but unlike mousses—which contain conditioners—the spray won't make your hair shiny.

CAUTION: Hair sprays may contain flammable gases as a propellent. Never use a spray in the presence of a lit match, a cigarette, a cigarette lighter, or any other open flame. If you plan to use a hair dryer, wait a few minutes after spraying to allow the gases to dissipate and the alcohol in the spray to evaporate.

■■   PROTEIN SHAMPOO   ■■

WHAT TO USE INSTEAD

Regular shampoo, plus a fresh egg or dried egg powder. Add one fresh egg or 2½ tablespoons dried egg powder to one cup of your regular shampoo. Mix thoroughly and use. The protein in the egg will fill in the chinks in every hair shaft to make your hair look fuller and smoother.

CAUTION: Do not store leftovers. The shampoo does not have enough preservative to protect it from bacterial contamination once you add the egg.

■■   SHAMPOO   ■■

WHAT TO USE INSTEAD

Bar soap.   Use this only when you have no other alternative. Unlike shampoos, bar soaps will leave an alkaline residue on your hair. To get rid of this sticky film, use an acid and water rinse: lemon juice for blonds, vinegar for brunets.

NOTES: YOUR OWN ALTERNATIVES

_____

_____

_____

_____

_____

_____

_____

_____

_____

_____

_____

_____

_____

_____

_____

_____

_____

_____

_____

_____

_____

_____

HEALTH CARE

This is an elastic category
that can stretch to cover everything
from an ice pack for your muscle ache
to an aspirin for your cold.
When looking for alternatives,
use caution and common sense.
A "cure" that works for others
may not work for you,
and some products are so special
that nothing else will do.
There is *no* acceptable substitute
for a contraceptive product
or for *any* drug prescribed
especially for you.
When in doubt,
check with your doctor.

■■   **ANTACIDS**   ■■

WHAT TO USE INSTEAD

Baking soda (sodium bicarbonate).   Sodium bicarbonate is
the active ingredient in many over-the-counter antacids.
Why pay for the tablet and the wrapping when you can have
yours straight from the box, 1 teaspoon in an 8-ounce glass of
water, for pennies a glass?

CAUTION: Bicarbonates may be hazardous under certain
conditions. People who have kidney disease or impaired kidney function, hypertension, heart disease, or any condition
that calls for a low-sodium diet, and people under a doctor's
care or taking any medication should check with their physician before using this substitute.

DO NOT use baking powder instead. Baking powder, which
is sodium bicarbonate plus cream of tartar, will not work as
an antacid.

■■   **CALAMINE LOTION**   ■■

WHAT TO USE INSTEAD

Baking soda (sodium bicarbonate).   To relieve the itch of a
mosquito bite, make a paste of baking soda and water and
dot it on the bite.

An ice cube.   Apply the ice cube to the mosquito bite for a
minute, being careful to remove it before the cold can freeze
your skin. The cold cube will overload the nerve endings in
your skin that tell your brain the bite is itching and the itch
will go away for a while.

■■ CALCIUM SUPPLEMENTS ■■

WHAT TO USE INSTEAD

A calcium carbonate antacid. Calcium carbonate, a form of calcium commonly found in over-the-counter calcium supplements, is also an antacid ingredient commonly found in OTC antacid tablets. For example, one regular Tums tablet has 500 mg calcium carbonate, about 63% of the RDA (800 mg) for a healthy adult.

Milk. One 8-ounce glass of whole milk has 272 mg calcium, one-third of the RDA for a healthy adult; an 8-ounce glass of low-fat (1% fat) milk has 281 mg calcium.

■■ COLD REMEDIES ■■

WHAT TO USE INSTEAD

Chicken soup. The steam will make your nose run more freely so you can blow out the mucus. A second benefit: chicken soup, which is often heavily salted, is one of the few foods you can still taste when you have a cold.

Spicy food. Spicy food (which is to say, food made with pepper) appears to irritate the membranes inside your nose and throat so that they "weep" a watery secretion that helps liquify mucus which make it easier for you to cough it up or blow it out.

■■ DENTAL FLOSS ■■

WHAT TO USE INSTEAD

White cotton thread. Thread is not as strong as dental

floss, but it works in a pinch. Just be sure to use thread that is narrow enough to fit between your teeth but not so sharp that it cuts the gum.

DO NOT use nylon thread. It is *very* sharp.

■■   EYEWASH   ■■

WHAT TO USE INSTEAD

Cool water.   The cool water may constrict the blood vessels that make your eyes red after a late night.

CAUTION: If symptoms persist or if you have pain and blurred vision, seek medical help *immediately*.

DO NOT use any other ingredient, except as directed by your doctor.

■■   HEATING PAD   ■■

WHAT TO USE INSTEAD

A terry wash-cloth, soaked in hot water and wrung out as much as possible.   The towel won't hold the heat for very long but can be useful when you have no heating pad. Always wear rubber gloves while wringing out, and make certain the towel is *not* scalding hot when applied to skin.

Cold pack.   Cold may be as useful as heat in relieving joint pain, according to the Arthritis Foundation. The effect varies from person to person; it works for some people but not for others. The best kind of cold pack is the "gel pack" that you store in the freezer and then use as needed. It doesn't chill your skin as severely as an ice cube or ice pack. Thus, it is unlikely to freeze or otherwise injure your skin.

■■   HUMIDIFIER   ■■

WHAT TO USE INSTEAD

A wide flat bowl filled with fresh water.   If possible, put the bowl on top of a radiator; the warmth will help the moisture evaporate even faster into the dry air. Be sure to empty the bowl and wash it thoroughly once a day to prevent the growth of micro-organisms in the water.

Potted houseplants.   The moisture evaporating from the plant, the soil, or pebbles in the saucer on which the pot rests can help humidify any room.

■■   ICE BAG / ICE PACK   ■■

WHAT TO USE INSTEAD

A plastic bag of frozen peas.   That's the Arthritis Foundation's ingenious substitute. This convenient "cold pack" has the distinct advantage of conforming to the shape of a joint or body part.

■■   MOUTHWASH   ■■

WHAT TO USE INSTEAD

Toothpaste.   Swish it around in your mouth.

Hydrogen peroxide.   As an occasional substitute for mouthwash, you can stir 1 teaspoon 3 percent hydrogen peroxide antiseptic into a full glass of water and swish it around in your mouth. **DO NOT** use this as your regular mouthwash; the peroxide can upset the natural balance of microorganisms in your mouth, encouraging the growth of a fungus that produces a condition known as "black, hairy tongue" because that's exactly what it looks like.

Salt-and-water gargle.   A gargle of 1 teaspoon salt in an 8-ounce glass of warm water can freshen your mouth. If you find the taste unpleasant, rinse afterwards with plain warm water.

■■   SUNBURN CREAM   ■■

WHAT TO USE INSTEAD

A cool bath or cool water compresses.   Either will soothe the pain of sunburned skin.

Cool sweet cream.   At first, sunburned skin is red and swollen. As it begins to heal, the swelling goes down and the skin shrinks, dries, and eventually peels. As it shrinks, it dries and itches. Sweet cream, which is a fat-and-water emulsion, can make the skin less dry, soothing the itch. To get the best effect, smooth on the cream, let it sit for a while, then rinse it off with cool water. This last step is *very* important; if you don't rinse well, the cream will eventually dry and flake on your skin, making it even more itchy.

CAUTION: These home remedies are meant to be used only on minor sunburn. A severe sunburn is an injury that may require medical treatment. If your sunburn is blistered or very painful, don't treat it yourself. Call your doctor.

■■   TOOTH PASTE/POWDER   ■■

WHAT TO USE INSTEAD

Baking soda or table salt.   These will get your teeth clean, but they won't protect you against cavities as a fluoridated dentifrice does. If you wear dentures or have extensive gum loss due to periodontal disease, check with your dentist before using these alternatives, which may be too abrasive for your teeth.

■■   VAGINAL DOUCHE   ■■

WHAT TO USE INSTEAD

Vinegar.   According to the FDA Advisory Panel on Over-the-Counter Contraceptives and Other Vaginal Products, a douche made of 1 ½ teaspoons distilled white vinegar in a quart of warm water is safe and effective in encouraging the growth of the beneficial microorganisms in the vagina. It's also additive-free and cheaper than a commercial douche preparation.

CAUTION: If there is redness, persistent itching, pain, or swelling, consult your doctor before using any douche.

NOTES: YOUR OWN ALTERNATIVES

_____

_____

_____

_____

_____

_____

_____

_____

_____

_____

_____

_____

_____

_____

_____

_____

_____

_____

_____

_____

_____

_____

_____

_____

_____

_____

_____

_____

_____

SKIN CARE

Like hair care,
skin care is fun and games
for kitchen chemists
who know that good food
is good *on* your skin
as well as in your diet.
And for the penny-pinchers
among us,
there's profit in making
skin creams do double
and maybe even triple duty
as a makeup remover and
a substitute for shaving cream
as well as a skin softener.

■■ ASTRINGENTS ■■

WHAT TO USE INSTEAD

Rubbing alcohol or witch hazel.   Astringents (which are sometimes known as "skin fresheners") are perfumed liquids you splash on after shaving or washing. They contain mild irritants such as aluminum salts that make your skin tingle and swell slightly so that your pores look smaller and your face is temporarily smoother and "fresher." Rubbing alcohol and witch hazel also have astringent properties. They can be used alone or mixed half-and-half with fresh cold water.

Cold water or an ice cube.   Splash on the water or run the cube *quickly* over your face (Don't hold it against your skin, lest you freeze!). Like astringents, the cold water or the ice cube will make your skin swell slightly so that your pores look smaller temporarily.

■ CLEANSING CREAM / ■
■ COLD CREAM ■

WHAT TO USE INSTEAD

Mineral oil or vegetable oil.   Either one is a handy, inexpensive substitute for cleansing cream.

Hardened vegetable oil (such as Crisco).   Another time-honored substitute for cleansing cream.

Any hand or body lotion.   In a pinch, a hand or body lotion can also be used to wipe away makeup.

■■   CLEANSING GRAINS   ■■

WHAT TO USE INSTEAD

Cornmeal or oatmeal, plus soap.   In a small saucepan (or in your microwave oven) bring 2 tablespoons of water to a boil. Add 2 teaspoons cornmeal or old-fashioned oatmeal (not instant/quick-cooking oatmeal). Cook the cereal until it is thick, then set it aside to cool. While it's cooling, soap up your hands with your regular toilet soap, then mix some of the cereal into the soapy foam and wash your face gently with the cereal-soap combination. Rinse thoroughly and pat dry with a soft cloth. **DO NOT** use on irritated or "broken out" skin.

A soft washcloth.   Either wash with the cloth, rubbing gently, or rub the dry cloth very gently over your face to wipe off the dead dry cells that pile up naturally on the surface of the skin.

■■   CUTICLE REMOVER   ■■

WHAT TO USE INSTEAD

Vegetable oils.   Cuticle remover is an alkali that softens keratin, the protein that composes the cuticle, so you can push the cuticle back from the nail. Vegetable oils will do the same thing. To make a softening solution, add a teaspoon of the oil or dishwashing liquid to a cup of warm water and soak your hands for a few minutes before manicuring your nails.

Soapy water.   Soap also softens keratin. Soaking your hands in a solution of warm water and bath soap is a fine way to start a manicure. It's also cheap.

■■   EYE MAKEUP REMOVER   ■■

WHAT TO USE INSTEAD

Mineral oil.   Mineral oil, the active ingredient in commercial eye makeup removers, effectively dissolves the shellacs that make waterproof mascaras water-repellent so that you can easily wipe them away.

Petroleum jelly (Vaseline).   Like mineral oil, petroleum jelly will dissolve eye makeup, but it's stickier and harder to get off your eyes. This is an acceptable alternative but not the preferred one.

■■   MOISTURIZERS   ■■

WHAT TO USE INSTEAD

Petroleum jelly (Vaseline) or mineral oil.   Petroleum jelly and mineral oil are extraordinarily effective moisturizers. They form a protective barrier that keeps water from evaporating from the surface of your skin. They're great if you plan to go out running on a cold day and you can use them as night creams, but they are too sticky to use during the day.

■■   NAIL CREAM   ■■

WHAT TO USE INSTEAD

Olive oil or petroleum jelly (Vaseline).   As a general rule, nails split because they lack water and are dry. Nail creams are designed to form a protective layer that will hold water in the nails and make them supple again. Massaging your nails with olive oil or petroleum jelly will do the same thing.

CAUTION: Brittle nails may be a symptom of a dietary or systemic problem. If your nails keep breaking or peeling despite the oil treatment, check with your doctor.

■ ■   SHAVING CREAM   ■ ■

WHAT TO USE INSTEAD

Hand or body lotion.   The formula for a hand or body lotion is similar to the formula for a brushless shaving cream. And the lotion—which leaves a smooth, protective film on your skin—is particularly good for shaving your legs.

■ ■   SKIN CLARIFIERS   ■ ■

(Skin clarifiers, which are sometimes called clarifying masques or exfoliating lotions, are designed to remove the top layer of dead cells constantly flaking off the surface of your skin. They leave your face temporarily smoother and softer.)

WHAT TO USE INSTEAD

A soft terry washcloth.   Rub gently against your skin.

NOTES: YOUR OWN ALTERNATIVES

_____

_____

_____

_____

_____

_____

_____

_____

_____

_____

_____

_____

_____

_____

_____

_____

_____

_____

_____

_____

_____

_____

_____

_____

_____

_____

HOUSEHOLD
AIDS

CLEANERS & CHEMICALS

If you're planning to run
away to a desert island
and can only haul along
one household chemical,
take chlorine bleach.
On its own
or mixed with water,
this wonder worker
can substitute for everything
except metal polish
and oven cleaners.
Tuck a box of baking soda
in your backpack and
you'll have it all.

■■ AIR FRESHENERS ■■

WHAT TO USE INSTEAD

Spray perfume or cologne.

Herbs and spices.   Fill a large flat, open bowl with herbs and spices. Over a few days it will perfume your room.

A baking apple.   Core a large Rome Beauty apple (don't go all the way through to the bottom; leave a layer of apple flesh and skin at the bottom). Peel away a ring of apple skin around the top to prevent the apple from bursting as it cooks. Put the apple in a baking dish. Fill the hollow in the apple with brown sugar. Dust on a pinch of cinnamon or allspice. Pour ½ cup water over the top of the apple, letting it seep into the sugared hollow and run down over the sides. Put the apple in a 350° F oven and let it cook until the skin is browning and the flesh feels soft when you pierce the skin with a cake-tester. The warm and spicy aroma is penetrating enough to make your home smell delicious. Best of all, you get to eat the apple afterward.

Cinnamon.   To dispel kitchen odors, simmer 1 ½ teaspoons of ground cinnamon in a cup of water for a few minutes.

Kitchen matches.   Light a kitchen match and hold it over the toilet bowl for a few seconds to get rid of unpleasant odors in the bathroom.

■■ ALUMINUM CLEANER ■■

WHAT TO USE INSTEAD

Very fine steel wool or sandpaper.   To shine brushed aluminum, rub gently with the steel wool or sandpaper.

A cut lemon.   To shine smooth aluminum, rub with the cut side of the lemon.

Vinegar.   To remove stains from the inside of either a brushed or smooth aluminum pot, fill the pot with a solution of 3 tablespoons vinegar to a pint of water and boil until the stain disappears. Replenish as needed.

■■   **BRASS POLISH**   ■■

WHAT TO USE INSTEAD

All-purpose metal cleaner, such as Noxon.   Use this to polish unlacquered brass.

Lemon and salt.   Use this to clean unlacquered brass. Cut a lemon in half, dip the cut side in salt or salt dissolved in warm vinegar, and rub the lemon over the brass. Then rinse off the lemon juice with cool water and polish the brass with a soft, lint-free cloth.

Nail polish remover.   To remove damaged lacquer coating, rub the brass with nail polish remover (acetone or amyl acetate). Then polish the brass or have it professionally relacquered.

■■   **CARPET SHAMPOO**   ■■

WHAT TO USE INSTEAD

Cornstarch.   Cornstarch is an absorbent powder that will pick up grease and dirt from your carpet. To clean the carpet, sprinkle on the cornstarch, leave it there for five minutes or so, then vacuum thoroughly.

█ █   CHROMIUM POLISH   █ █

WHAT TO USE INSTEAD

Silver polish. This non-abrasive cleaner will shine the chromium without scratching it.

Vinegar. Apply the vinegar with a paper towel and polish with a dry towel or lint-free cloth to make the chromium shine.

Neither of these simple cleaners will shine chromium that looks rusted. Chromium doesn't rust; what you're seeing is a place on the pipe or faucet where the chromium plating has worn away and the metal underneath has rusted. You can clean off the rust with naval jelly, but to restore the shine you must have the metal professionally re-chromed.

█ █   CLOSET DEODORIZERS   █ █

WHAT TO USE INSTEAD

Cedar chips, blocks, and shavings; cedar hangers, cedar shoe trees, or cedar oil. The chips and blocks may be available at your local lumber yard. If not, you can order them from L. L. Bean (1-800-341-4341) or Orvis (1-802-362-1300), who also sell the hangers and shoe trees. L. L. Bean also sells shaving-filled refills for pet beds. You can tear open the refill sack and use the shavings to make your own cedar sachets.

Pomander balls. Take a large, firm, fresh orange and stick whole cloves into the peel until the whole orange is covered with the cloves. Then roll the orange in ground cinnamon and allspice until it is completely covered with a dusting of the spices. Wrap the orange in tissue paper and let it sit on a shelf in your kitchen until it dries and shrinks. When it has dried, take off the paper, dust off any loose spice powder and hang the pomander in your closet. The scent will be divine.

■■   **COFFEEPOT CLEANER**   ■■

WHAT TO USE INSTEAD

Dishwashing liquids or soap pads.   Both will clean the pot and remove the coffee oils that can spoil the flavor of the next cup you brew.

Vinegar.   To freshen a coffeepot, run it through its cycle filled with water plus 1 tablespoon of white distilled vinegar.

■■   **COPPER POLISH**   ■■

WHAT TO USE INSTEAD

Buttermilk, yogurt, lemon juice, or vinegar.   All three are natural acids that will clean and shine unlacquered copper. Rub them on the copper with a soft cloth or paper towel. When the copper is clean, rinse it thoroughly with cool water; then rub copper dry to prevent water spots.

White flour, salt, and vinegar or lemon juice.   To clean unlacquered copper, make a paste of equal parts white flour, salt, and vinegar or lemon juice. Rub the paste onto the copper with a soft cloth or paper towel. When the copper is clean and shiny, rinse the paste off with cool water then rub dry the copper thoroughly to prevent water spots.

Toothpaste.   Apply with a damp cloth or paper towel to unlacquered copper, as above. Don't use the abrasive toothpastes or powders designed to take stains off your teeth; they may scratch the copper.

Soapy water and ammonia.   To remove "green rust" from

unlacquered copper, wash the copper in a solution of 1 table-spoon ammonia to a quart of warm, soapy water. Then rinse thoroughly and dry to prevent water spots.

To clean *lacquered* copper, simply wipe with a damp cloth. For stubborn grease residue or spots, use warm soapy water.

■■   DISHWASHING LIQUID   ■■

WHAT TO USE INSTEAD

A stiff-bristled vegetable brush and hot water.   Soak the dishes to loosen dried food, then brush well under hot running water.

Liquid hand soap.   An expensive alternative to be used only when you really need help in a hurry.

CAUTION: Do not reverse the substitution and use dishwashing liquid instead of bath soap or shampoo because the dishwashing liquid contains chemical cleaners and brighteners that may irritate your skin when you use it day after day. (That's why so many people wear protective gloves when washing dishes.)

■■   DISINFECTANT CLEANSER   ■■

WHAT TO USE INSTEAD

Chlorine bleach.   Make a solution of chlorine bleach and water, 1 ounce (⅛ cup) bleach per quart of warm water. This solution will clean and disinfect sinks, bathtubs, ceramic tile, linoleum, and porcelain and enameled surfaces, leaving a distinctive odor that some people find familiar and pleasing. (It also kills mold, cold.)

■■ DRAIN CLEANER ■■

WHAT TO USE INSTEAD

Hot water.   To keep drains from clogging, run the hot water in the kitchen sink for a few minutes after you finish doing the dishes. The water may help flush away debris that has slipped into the drain and/or dissolve and wash away fats than can harden and clog the drain. Once the drain is stopped up, though, there is no really effective alternative to a chemical drain cleaner or a mechanical snake.

DO NOT use salt or coffee grounds. Salt is ineffective; coffee grounds can stuff up the drain.

■■ DUST SPRAY ■■

WHAT TO USE INSTEAD

A dustcloth or mop moistened with plain, cool water.   Dust sprays are aerosol oil sprays that damp dust down so that it doesn't go floating off into the air. A damp mop or dustcloth will do exactly the same thing.

■■ FLOOR POLISH REMOVER ■■

WHAT TO USE INSTEAD

All-purpose household cleaner (such as Spic and Span) or a solution of ammonia and water.   To clean the wax off linoleum or floor tiles, prepare a solution of household cleaner and water or ammonia and water as directed on the box or bottle and wash the floor. **DO NOT** use this solution on polished wood floors.

■■   FURNITURE POLISH   ■■

WHAT TO USE INSTEAD

Olive oil.   To polish wood that has been stained but not lac-quered or painted. Spread a little olive oil on the wood; then rub hard with a soft, lint-free cloth until the wood is shiny and smooth, without a trace of stickiness.

Mild soap and water or plain water.   For any plasticized surface: formica, vinyl, or a wood that has been lacquered, painted, shellacked or urethaned.

■■   GLASS CLEANER   ■■

WHAT TO USE INSTEAD

Distilled white vinegar and water.   Wash glass or crystal tumblers or plates in hot soapy water, then rinse in a solution of one quart cool water plus a half-cup vinegar.

■■   HOUSEHOLD CLEANSER   ■■

WHAT TO USE INSTEAD

Baking soda (sodium bicarbonate).   A solution of 2 table-spoons sodium bicarbonate dissolved in 1 quart warm water will clean plaster, tile, and porcelain surfaces.

Ammonia and water.   Prepare a solution as directed on the bottle. This is especially good on tile surfaces. Use protective gloves when working with an ammonia solution; the chemical may irritate your skin.

■■   MOLD STAIN REMOVER   ■■

WHAT TO USE INSTEAD

Chlorine bleach.   A solution of chlorine bleach and water, prepared as directed on the bottle, will kill mold and remove stains from bathroom tiles. Use protective gloves when cleaning with chlorine bleach; the chemical may irritate your skin.

Scouring powder and water.   Mix to a paste, and apply with a toothbrush to scrub away the stains on grout between the tiles.

■■   OVEN CLEANER   ■■

WHAT TO USE INSTEAD

Baking soda (sodium bicarbonate).   Add enough water to make a paste. Spread the paste on the cool oven surface and let it sit overnight, if necessary. Then scrub it off with the plastic mesh sponge you use to clean nonstick pans. The sponge won't scratch the oven's porcelain surface, but it should take off the dirt and debris. Repeat the process until the oven is clean; then wipe the surface with clear water to remove any traces of the cleaner.

DO NOT use scouring pads. The steel wool may scratch the porcelain.

■■   PAINTBRUSH CLEANER   ■■

WHAT TO USE INSTEAD

All-purpose household cleaner (such as Spic and Span) or

laundry detergent.   As soon as you have finished painting, put the wet brush to soak in a thick solution of detergent and water (½ cup detergent per quart of water). It may take a while (sometimes days), but this solution will eventually clean even brushes saturated with oil-based paints.

Rubbing alcohol (isopropyl alcohol).   This solvent dissolves shellac and shellac-based primers.

■■   PAINT   REMOVER   ■■

WHAT TO USE INSTEAD

Nail polish remover.   To pick up spatters of dry paint on a wood floor, rub the spot gently with a cloth or tissue dipped in nail polish remover. (Remember that the solvents in the remover will also dissolve a urethane, shellac or paint coating on the floor.)

Fine steel wool or sandpaper.   This will smooth away dry paint spots on wood or unlacquered metal. Rub gently. If the wood has been sealed with urethane, shellac or any other protective coating, rubbing may also remove some of the coating.

■■   PLASTIC GLUE   ■■

WHAT TO USE INSTEAD

Nail polish remover.   Acetone and amyl acetate, the solvents in nail polish removers, dissolve and soften plastics. If you paint nail polish remover on two pieces of plastic and then press the wet surfaces together, the plastics should bond together as they dry.

■■ REFRIGERATOR DEODORIZER ■■

WHAT TO USE INSTEAD

Baking soda (sodium bicarbonate).   Baking soda absorbs odors which dissipate when the bicarbonate eventually decomposes. Just open the box and place it on your refrigerator shelf. Write the date on the box and then replace the baking soda every three months or so.

DO NOT use baking powder. This mixture of baking soda and cream of tartar does not contain enough baking soda to do the job properly.

■■ SACHET ■■

WHAT TO USE INSTEAD

Your usual bath soap.   The soap will perfume your dresser drawer and, since you use it every day, you know you aren't sensitive to the fragrance. And, if you run out of soap, you always know there's a spare in the drawer.

■■ SCOURING PADS ■■

WHAT TO USE INSTEAD

A stiff-bristle vegetable brush.   Scrub the food off dishes and pots under hot running water.

Fine steel wool.   Use the steel wool as is or saturate it with your regular dishwashing liquid. This is an expensive but useful substitute for people who are sensitive to the detergents in scouring pads. Throw out the steel wool pad after you finish the dishes. Since it hasn't got the rust retardents found in regular scouring pads, this substitute pad will rust practically before your eyes.

CAUTION: Always wear protective gloves to avoid getting steel splinters in your fingers.

■■   SCOURING POWDER   ■■

WHAT TO USE INSTEAD

Baking soda (sodium bicarbonate).   Use exactly as you would a scouring powder. It will clean pots and pans, dishes, and even the kitchen sink. Because the sodium bicarbonate is less abrasive than regular scouring powder, you can also use it to clean the porcelain surface of your stove, refrigerator, and appliances.

■■   SILICONE SPRAY   ■■

WHAT TO USE INSTEAD

A cake of bath soap or a wax candle.   To make a drawer or door slide closed more easily; rub the soapcake or the wax candle over the drawer runner or the edge of the door. (This won't work if the door or drawer is clearly warped out of shape or very swollen by excess humidity.)

■■   SILVER POLISH   ■■

WHAT TO USE INSTEAD

Soap and water plus baking soda (sodium bicarbonate).   The baking soda is a mild abrasive that will clean the silver without scratching it.

DO NOT use an all-purpose metal polish or polishes meant for other metals. They are all too abrasive for silver, which is a very soft metal that scratches easily.

■■   STAINLESS STEEL POLISH   ■■

WHAT TO USE INSTEAD

Warm soapy water. Clean the steel surface with a nonscratch, plastic mesh sponge, rinse thoroughly under cool running water, and dry the object immediately to prevent water spots.

Silver polish or all-purpose metal polish (such as Noxon). The silver polish, which is nonabrasive, is preferable for smooth stainless flatware, pots, and pans. Other polishes may scratch a smooth surface, but they are fine for a brushed surface.

DO NOT use scouring pads. The steel wool will scratch the surface of smooth stainless steel.

■■   TOILET-BOWL CLEANER   ■■

WHAT TO USE INSTEAD

All-purpose household cleaner (such as Spic and Span). Make a solution as directed on the package.

Baking soda (sodium bicarbonate). Baking soda is a nonabrasive scouring cleanser.

Chlorine bleach. Pour ½ cup bleach into the bowl; let it sit for half an hour; then scrub. The bleach will deodorize the bowl as well as clean it. Wear protective gloves when cleaning with chlorine bleach; the chemical can irritate your skin.

DO NOT use scouring powder. The abrasive powder will scratch the surface of the bowl allowing dirt and microorganisms to grow inside.

■■ TUB AND TILE CLEANER ■■

WHAT TO USE INSTEAD

Chlorine bleach. Dilute as directed on the container and use to scrub down tub and tiles. The solution will wipe away mold as well as grime. Wear protective gloves when cleaning with chlorine bleach; the chemical can irritate your skin.

Cream of tartar and hydrogen peroxide. Mix the two to make a paste. Apply the paste with a stiff brush and scrub the tile or tub. (Use the 3 percent hydrogen peroxide sold as an antiseptic, **not** the 10 percent "bleaching" peroxide.)

Lemons. Rub a cut lemon on the porcelain to bleach out rust stains around the drain pipe.

Soapsuds and ammonia. Make a solution of ammonia and soapy water as directed on the container and use it as a bleach to wash away green copper stains around drain pipes. Wear protective gloves when cleaning with an ammonia solution; the chemical can irritate your skin.

CAUTION: *Never* combine ammonia with a product that contains chlorine bleach. The combination will liberate extremely poisonous chlorine gas fumes.

■■ WALLPAPER CLEANER ■■

WHAT TO USE INSTEAD

For vinyl wallpaper: A mild soap and water solution.

For plain, uncoated paper: An art gum eraser or a wadded piece of white bread to rub away stains.

DO NOT use this on flocked wallpapers.

■■   **WHITE PASTE/GLUE**   ■■

WHAT TO USE INSTEAD

Flour-and-water paste.   This time-honored substitute will hold small pieces of paper or wood together for a while.

■■   **WINDOW CLEANER**   ■■

WHAT TO USE INSTEAD

Ammonia.   Add 1 tablespoon to a quart of warm water. Wear protective gloves when cleaning with an ammonia solution; the chemical may irritate your skin.

Distilled white vinegar.   Add half a cup of vinegar to a quart of water and use the solution to clean the windows.

Rubbing alcohol (isopropyl alcohol).   In cold weather, add 3 tablespoons to a quart of water. The alcohol acts as an anti-freeze, helping to keep your windows free of frost.

Tissue paper.   To polish clean windows, rub with a piece of the stiff white tissue paper used to wrap gifts.

NOTES: YOUR OWN ALTERNATIVES

_____

_____

_____

INSECT REPELLENTS
& BUG KILLERS

What you want
are cheap, safe,
effective alternatives
to organic chemicals.
What you get is
Mother Nature's
own insecticidal plants—
marigolds, onions or radishes—
or even wood shavings
for moths.

■■   CRAWLING-BUG KILLER   ■■

WHAT TO USE INSTEAD

Boric acid.   This works best against roaches and other insects crawling around under your sink. Sprinkle the boric acid around drains and in the corners. The roaches will track through it, then lick it off their feet and expire back in their nests.

CAUTION: Boric acid is a poison; keep it out of the reach of children and pets.

■■   GARDEN PESTICIDES   ■■

WHAT TO USE INSTEAD

In the garden: Plant onions, marigolds, radishes, or nasturtiums in your flower or truck garden.   Each of these plants repels aphids and other insects.

On houseplants: A mild soap-and-water solution.   Wash your houseplants once a week to remove pests and/or their eggs from leaves and flowers.

■■   MILDEW PREVENTIVES   ■■

(Mildew is a mold that grows on fabrics, leather, wood, and paper stored in warm, damp, airless places. Mildew preventives contain chemicals such as paraformaldehyde biphenyls or 1,1,1-trichroroethane that kill the mold.)

WHAT TO USE INSTEAD

Fresh air.   The drier and airier the surface, the less likely it is to support the growth of mold.

A light bulb.   To prevent mold and mildew in a damp closet, turn on the closet light and leave it burning for an hour or two.

CAUTION: The bulb must be at least 12 inches from any clothes, plastic bags, or other material that might burn or melt if heated. NEVER close the closet door while the light is on. NEVER go out of the house and leave the bulb burning in your absence.

■■ MOTH BALLS/FLAKES ■■

(Mothballs and flakes may contain either naphthalene or paradichlorobenzene, poisonous chemicals that release irritating fumes.)

WHAT TO USE INSTEAD

Cedar wood.   Cedar, which smells good and is nonpoisonous, is reputed to repel moths and other insects. You can get your cedar in blocks, chips, shavings, hangers, drawer liners, or shoe trees, all by mail, from L. L. Bean (1-800-341-4341) or Eddie Bauer (1-800-426-8020).

Clothes brush.   Basic but effective. Delicate moth eggs are destroyed by vigorous brushing. Brush often to protect your clothes without chemicals.

■■ ROACH REPELLENT ■■

WHAT TO USE INSTEAD

Bay leaves.   In 1982, researchers at Kansas State University were able to validate this folk remedy by showing that bay leaves repelled cockroaches in insect tanks. The active ingredient in the leaves is cineaole (also known as eucalyptol). A bay leaf in your flour canister should keep the flour free of bugs.

CAUTION: Keep bay leaves out of reach of children or pets. If swallowed, whole leaves or leaves broken in pieces may block an airway or obstruct the intestines.

NOTES: YOUR OWN ALTERNATIVES

_____

_____

_____

_____

_____

_____

_____

_____

_____

_____

_____

_____

_____

_____

_____

_____

_____

LAUNDRY &
CLOTHING CARE

Unless you plan to put your
clothes in the stream
to get them clean,
you'll have to invest in
a laundry detergent.
Any good one can do the wash,
presoak stains, brighten colors, and
spot-clean many washable fabrics.
Which one's best for you?
The one whose fragrance
(or lack of it) you like.
No matter what Madison Avenue
says, everything else is
pretty much the same.

■■   ANTISTATIC SPRAY   ■■

WHAT TO USE INSTEAD

Fabric softener.   Static electricity builds up in fabrics when the fabrics get very dry. Fabric softeners, like antistatic sprays, contain chemicals called *surfactants* that trap moisture on the surface of the fabric and help repel static electricity. For washable fabrics, the softeners are a less expensive alternative to the sprays.

Steam.   To add moisture to clothes made of washable fabrics, hang the dry clothes in the bathroom with the shower running hot enough to fill the room with steam. This may keep the clothes static free for a few hours.

■■   CLOTHES BRUSH   ■■

WHAT TO USE INSTEAD

Masking tape.   Wind the tape around your hand with the sticky side out, then run your hand slowly and gently over the garment. The tape will pick up pieces of dust, animal hair, and the like. A transparent tape (such as Scotch tape) is also useful, but it is so much narrower that you have to use more of it.

■■   LAUNDRY PRESOAK   ■■

WHAT TO USE INSTEAD

Detergent or soap powder.   Mix the detergent with just enough water to make a paste and spread the paste on shirt collars or other stained areas. Let the paste sit for 15 minutes, then launder as usual. (A paste made from a detergent such as Tide that has added bleach or brighteners should be used *only* on white fabrics. A plain soap powder such as Ivory Snow may be safe for colored fabrics—but try it first on a small, hidden spot and then check frequently to be sure the color is not fading.)

■■ LAUNDRY STARCH ■■

WHAT TO USE INSTEAD

Unflavored gelatine. Dissolve a packet of unflavored gelatine in a quart of warm water. Then dilute this solution with a second quart of warm water and use the liquid as a stiffening bath for delicate washable fabrics such as thin cotton. Iron while damp.

■■ LEATHER CONDITIONER ■■

WHAT TO USE INSTEAD

Castor oil. This substitute works well on unpolished, dark-leather shoes. Once or twice a year, spread the oil on the shoes, then rub hard with a clean, soft lint-free cloth until the leather shines and feels smooth to the touch, without a trace of stickines.

DO NOT use castor oil on pale-leather shoes; the oil may leave dark spots.

Hand lotion. Smooth the lotion on patent leather belts, handbags, or shoes, then rub gently with a soft tissue, paper towel, or cloth towel to clean the patent leather and get rid of the stickiness.

CAUTION: Use hand lotion on patent leather *only*.

■■   SHOE POLISH   ■■

WHAT TO USE INSTEAD

Petroleum jelly (Vaseline).   For patent leather and unpolished dark-leather shoes. Rub the jelly on and then polish the shoes with a lint-free cloth until all the stickiness is gone.

DO NOT use petroleum jelly on light-color leather shoes; the oil will stain the leather.

DO NOT use it on shoes that have been polished; the oil may dissolve the wax or liquid polish, leaving a mottled surface. If you really want to give it a try, rub it on a small, inconspicuous spot first to see if it cleans without spotting.

Black wax polish, neutral polish, saddle soap.   Use these as a substitute for brown, blue, or cordovan polish. Neutral polishes and saddle soap will work on any color leather shoes since they clean but don't recolor rubbed spots. A black wax polish rubbed on a blue or brown shoe will deepen the original color of the leather, not change it dramatically.

DO NOT use a black *liquid* polish. Wax polishes are transluscent; the original color of the leather will come through. Liquid polishes, on the other hand, form an opaque protective film. They will change the color of the shoe.

■■   SILICONE SHOE SPRAY   ■■

WHAT TO USE INSTEAD

Wax shoe polish or saddle soap.   To make leather shoes and boots water-resistant, polish them with several coats of wax or saddle soap. Be sure to rub well with a lint-free cloth between coats of polish to avoid sticky wax build-up.

Petroleum jelly.   To waterproof unpolished dark-leather shoes or boots, polish with a coat of white petroleum jelly (Vaseline is the best-known brand), rubbing well with a lint-free cloth until there is absolutely no hint of stickiness.

■■   SPOT REMOVER   ■■

WHAT TO USE INSTEAD

Ammonia and water.   For bloodstains. Wear protective gloves when cleaning with an ammonia solution; the chemical may irritate your skin.

Cornstarch.   For grease or oil stains. Shake on the cornstarch; let it dry; brush it off.

Laundry detergent.   Make a paste of detergent and water and use as a general spot remover for washable fabrics.

Laundry presoak.   For protein stains (blood, chocolate, meat, milk). Make a paste with water and use to bleach out the stain.

Peroxide.   For blood, chocolate, meat, or milk. Always use ordinary (3%) peroxide antiseptic, not bleaching peroxide, a stronger solution that may damage fabrics.

Rubbing alcohol (isopropyl alcohol).   For grass stains and dye stains.

Distilled white vinegar.   For jam, jelly, mustard, and wax stains.

CAUTION: All stain removers, including these substitutes, may change the color of fabrics on which they are used. Always try the remover on a small, hidden spot first to see if it bleaches or otherwise damages the fabric.

■■ SUEDE BRUSH ■■

WHAT TO USE INSTEAD

Masking tape or transparent tape (such as Scotch tape).   Wind the tape around your hand, sticky side out, and run it gently over the suede to pick up dust and dirt.

A cardboard emery board.   Rub the suede gently with the less abrasive side of the emery board to raise the nap. Never use a metal nail file; which can tear or damage suede.

NOTES: YOUR OWN ALTERNATIVES

_____

_____

_____

_____

_____

_____

_____

_____

_____

_____

_____

_____

PET & PLANT CARE

If you're the one
who pays the bills for Fido
and the ficus in the corner,
you know that pets and plants
are serious investments
that take lots of special
care and handling,
not to mention
lots of cold, hard cash.
So isn't it nice to know
you can beat the system
once in a while by sharing
your food and cosmetics?

■■   DOG FOOD   ■■

WHAT TO USE INSTEAD
Any dog foods marked "complete" will provide a balanced diet, with all the nutrients your dog needs. But the various kinds of food (dry, moist, semi-moist) differ in water content, which means they provide different amounts of calories per pound.

Food Type	Calories Per Pound*
Dry ("kibble")	1,400 - 1,600
Moist food (canned food)	500 - 700
Semimoist burgers	1,200 - 1,450

*The variation reflects different recipes from different manufacturers. Source: The Pet Food Institute, Washington, D.C.

As a general rule, small adult dogs need approximately 50 calories per pound per day; large dogs need about 20 calories per pound per day. According to The Pet Food Institute in Washington, a 5-pound adult toy poodle should get about 245 calories' worth of food a day, while an 180-pound Great Dane would require about 3,600 calories' worth.

While you (or your dog) may prefer one type of food to another, you can generally switch around with no problems. However, like people, dogs are individual and some may require special feeding. If so, check with your vet who can provide therapeutic formulas tailored to your pet's needs.

Table scraps.   Whether or not you should feed your dog table scraps is a matter of some disagreement among experts. Everyone agrees that table scraps should not be your dog's basic diet, but what about once in a while?

The consensus seems to be that while dog food is always a better bet than "people food," you *can* toss the dog a special treat on occasion. If you do, stick to simple foods such as plain cooked spaghetti, rice, vegetables, eggs, chicken, turkey, and trimmed meat or a small piece of fresh apple.

NEVER feed your pet fatty foods, milks, spicy foods, chocolate, rich desserts, and alcohol beverages or foods made with alcohol.

DO NOT give your pet bones. There's no bone, not even a beef bone, that cannot eventually be shattered by a dog's teeth. Feed a dog a bone and you're likely to end up with trouble. Rawhide and/or dog biscuits are a much safer bet.

■ ■   FLEA COLLARS   ■ ■

WHAT TO USE INSTEAD

A vacuum cleaner.   For the carpet and the furniture, of course, not the dog. City pets, who rarely get out into the underbrush, may pick up their fleas from colonies ensconced in your walls, floors, or furniture. Vacuum thoroughly to remove flea eggs and larvae, and you may be able to keep your animal flea-free. If your home or pet is already infested, don't waste your time with half-measures. Call a professional exterminator for the apartment and ship the dog or cat off to the vet for a professional debugging.

DO NOT use brewer's yeast. People who eat brewer's yeast produce a flea-repelling odor when the yeast is metabolized through sweat glands all over their bodies. But dogs have sweat glands only in their noses and on the pads of their feet, neither of which is attractive to fleas in the first place. Feeding dogs brewer's yeast won't protect them from fleas.

■■   KITTY LITTER   ■■

WHAT TO USE INSTEAD

Shredded newspapers. This classic substitute is not as absorbent as commercial kitty litter but is adequate in a pinch.

To deodorize regular kitty litter, stir half a cup of baking soda through the litter box.

■■   PET SHAMPOO   ■■

WHAT TO USE INSTEAD

Any mild shampoo. Hair is hair, and your pet's will come clean with any plain and simple shampoo without conditioners (which can make the dog's hair sticky) or coloring agents or antidandruff medication. If your dog's hair is long and tangles when you try to comb it out after the bath, ask your vet about the validity of a simple softening rinse (but *not* a sticky conditioner).

■■   PLANT FOOD   ■■

WHAT TO USE INSTEAD

Unflavored gelatine. Gelatine provides nitrogen, one of the three nutrients essential for healthy plant growth. (The other two are phosphorus and potassium.) Mix an envelope of unflavored gelatine (such as Knox Gelatine) with one cup (8 ounces) boiling water to dissolve the gelatine, add three cups (24 ounces) cool water. Once a month, water your plants with this solution rather than plain water. Discard leftovers; do not store the solution.

Used coffee grounds.   They're rich in potassium. Sprinkle them on the houseplant soil once in a while to encourage strong bud growth.

Mineral supplements.   To replace minerals lost from the soil, add a multimineral nutritional supplement tablet or capsule to a pot of soil and water thoroughly.

■■   **PLANT PESTICIDES**   ■■

WHAT TO USE INSTEAD

Soap and water.   Houseplants should be washed regularly in the tub under a warm, gentle shower (use a hair-spray nozzle) to wash away eggs or minor bug infestations. If the pests have moved in en masse, forget the shower and get pesticide designed to control the specific bug. Should that fail, discard the plant to protect the others in your home.

■■   **PLANT POLISH**   ■■

WHAT TO USE INSTEAD

Plain running water or warm water and mild soap. Houseplant "polishes" are emulsions of water and waxes or resins that dry to a shiny coat on the plant leaves. They're really not necessary, since a clean, healthy plant is naturally shiny. To keep your plants attractive (as well as discourage bugs), make it a habit from time to time to put the potted plant in the bathtub and wash it with a gentle spray from a shampooing hose. If it's really dirty, wash the leaves with a solution of mild soap and water, then rinse thoroughly with tepid water.

NOTES: YOUR OWN ALTERNATIVES

BEVERAGES

ALCOHOLIC
BEVERAGES & MIXERS

A substitute for champagne?
An alternative to aged port?
It's enough to trigger trauma
in those who live by the vintage charts.
Which may be you—until the night
you reach for the wine
for your veal Marsala and/or
the rum for your ice cream sauce
and find that the bottle is empty.
When that inevitable *crise de cuisine* occurs,
keep cool, keep an open mind,
grit your teeth, and try an alternative.
When it saves the day
(not to mention the dish),
accept the praise of your guests
in dignified silence.

■■ ALE ■■

WHAT TO USE INSTEAD

Beer. Ale and beer are beverages made by fermenting germinated (malted) barley and flavoring the beverage with the flowers of the hop plant, which gives the brew a slightly bitter flavor. There are technical differences in the ways the two are made that give ale a slightly more bitter flavor, but individual beers may actually have a wider range of flavor variations than a given beer and a given ale. In cooking, either one will do. What matters is the alcohol (which tenderizes meat) and the bitter hops (which give carbonnades—stews made with beer—their characteristic flavor).

■■ CALVADOS ■■

WHAT TO USE INSTEAD

Applejack. *Calvados* is the European name for apple brandy; *applejack,* the American name.

Apple cider, apple juice. These work well in cooking and marinades. The flavor may not be as intense as the flavor of calvados, but it's definitely apple.

■■ CHAMPAGNE ■■

WHAT TO USE INSTEAD

Sparkling white wines from any country. *Champagne* is the sparkling white or blush (pink) wine from the Champagne district of France. By tradition—and French law—no wine made anywhere else can be labeled "champagne," although it can carry the words *methode champenoise* (champagne method). When you're celebrating, however, any sparkling wine, sweet or dry as you prefer, will do as well.

White wine plus seltzer or club soda. As a substitute for champagne in cooking, mix one part wine with one part soda and use as directed in a recipe for a sauce or punch.

Ginger ale. This is, of course, the classic teetotaler's substitute for sweet champagne or sparkling wine in punches, cocktails, and cooking.

■■ "COOKING WINE" ■■

WHAT TO USE INSTEAD

The wines we drink. ("Cooking wines" are specific products, sweetened wines sold in grocery stores and meant for cooking, not drinking. They are generally inferior to the wines we drink.) Since cooking concentrates the flavor of wine, it makes a poor wine taste worse. Food cooked with wine tastes best when the wine is a good one. Which you choose depends on what you're cooking. Burgundies and Bordeaux are good in beef or chicken stews; Chianti tastes great in spaghetti sauce; dry white wines are good in fish sauces; sweet wines, such as cream sherry, are good in cream sauces.

■■ MARSALA ■■

WHAT TO USE INSTEAD

Dry ("cocktail") sherry. Marsala, which is rarely served as a beverage, is used in Italian cuisine. As a general rule, you can substitute a dry cocktail sherry, but it's a good idea to taste the dish before serving. Some Marsalas, like some sherries, are sweeter than others. If you're accustomed to a sweeter flavor than you get from the dry sherry, you may want to correct the seasoning with a pinch of sugar at the end.

■■ PORT ■■

WHAT TO USE INSTEAD

Cream sherry. Port and cream sherry are both fortified wines (wines to which brandy has been added). Both are sweet, rich and deep (although port is more intense and richer). Both are dessert wines that go well with fruit and cheese.

■■ RICE WINE ■■

WHAT TO USE INSTEAD

Dry sherry. In cooking, dry sherry can be substituted for Chinese rice wine in Oriental dishes.

■■ SAKE ■■

WHAT TO USE INSTEAD

Dry white wine or dry vermouth. The flavors are different, but these white wines work well in recipes made with sake.

■■ SHERRY ■■

WHAT TO USE INSTEAD

Madeira and Marsala wines. Like sherry, these fortified

wines (wines to which brandy has been added) can be used to flavor cream sauces and cream or clear soups. Taste the wine before you use it to be sure it's sweet (or dry), whichever you prefer. Like sherries, Madeiras and Marsalas vary in sweetness.

■■   SPARKLING WATERS   ■■

WHAT TO USE INSTEAD

Club soda, seltzer.   Seltzer is plain carbonated water. Club soda, which has a slight mineral flavor, is carbonated water plus salts (usually sodium bicarbonate). Either can be a satisfying, inexpensive substitute for pricey bottled naturally sparkling waters.

■■   TOMATO JUICE   ■■

WHAT TO USE INSTEAD

Tomato paste.   One 6-ounce can tomato paste plus three cans (18 ounces) water = 24 ounces tomato juice. To match the flavor of commercial tomato juice, add salt and sugar to taste.

Tomato sauce.   One 8-ounce can tomato sauce plus 8 ounces water = 16 ounces (2 cups/1 pint) tomato juice.

■■   WHITE WINE   ■■

WHAT TO USE INSTEAD

Dry vermouth.   In cooking, you can substitute dry vermouth for white wine. Since the vermouth is flavored with herbs, it's a good idea to check the seasoning before adding more.

Ginger ale or unsweetened white grape juice.   In cooking or in punches, you can substitute these for sweet sparkling or still white wine. To substitute the grape juice for a sparkling wine, use one part grape juice to one part seltzer or club soda.

■■   WINES   ■■

WHAT TO USE INSTEAD

The following wines are grouped together not because they taste exactly the same (they don't) but because they can be used with the same foods or in the same recipes:

Dry white wines: Chablis, brut champagne, chardonnay, folle blanche, pinot blanc.

Sweet white wines: Sec champagnes, Reisling, Rhine wine, sylvaner, traminer.

Dry red wines: Burgundy, gamay, pinot noir.

Sweet red wines: Claret, cabernet sauvignon, ruby cabernet, zinfandel.

White dessert wines: Sauterne, catawba, semillon.

Red dessert wines: Marsala, Madeira, port, sherry, Tokay.

NOTES: YOUR OWN ALTERNATIVES

_____

_____

_____

_____

COFFEE, TEA, & COCOA

These three
natural beverages—
our legacy, respectively,
from the Arabs, the Chinese,
and the Aztecs—
are all low-calorie,
high-power mood elevators,
and the most popular
legal stimulants around.

■■ COCOA ■■

WHAT TO USE INSTEAD

Carob powder. This chocolate substitute comes plain or in a "hot-drink" mix similar to cocoa mixes, complete with powdered milk and sweeteners. It's most valuable for people who are allergic to chocolate.

Plain chocolate bars (no nuts or cream fillings) or baking chocolate. Solid chocolate has much more fat than cocoa. When you dissolve an ounce of solid chocolate in a cup of hot water, you get an oily liquid. You can cut the oiliness a bit by mixing the chocolate and water in a blender with a teaspoon of powdered milk per cup of hot water.

The one exception to this rule is "drinking" chocolate, a solid bar made especially to be used in hot chocolate. These chocolate bars, which are sold primarily in Hispanic grocery stores or in supermarkets in Spanish-speaking neighborhoods, have much less fat than ordinary bars of chocolate, and they are sugared and spiced with a variety of flavorings, including cinnamon. When you bite into them, they taste dry and crumbly, but they dissolve into wonderful hot chocolate, an ounce of chocolate per cup. Brands to look for include Cortes (sweet and not very spicy), Goya (dark, sweet), and Menier (bittersweet, rich). To give the drink a little more zip, add a few grains of black or white ground pepper.

■■ COFFEE ■■

WHAT TO USE INSTEAD

Chicory. Roasted ground chicory, a bitter-tasting caffeine-free root, is sometimes added to coffee as an extender or to intensify the natural bitterness of the brew.

Cereal beverages. Nobody would ever mistake these sweet-tasting, caffeine-free beverages for coffee, but they *are* dark and hot and if you absolutely have to give up coffee (or if you're just looking for an occasional substitute), these may be the ticket. Postum is the granddaddy of the clan; health food stores and supermarkets now stock many other brands as well.

■■   ESPRESSO   ■■

WHAT TO USE INSTEAD

Regular coffee, brewed double strength. The usual coffee measure is 2 level tablespoons coffee for each 6 ounces of fresh cold water. To brew your regular coffee at espresso strength, use 4 level tablespoons per 6 ounces of water and serve each cup with a twist of lemon peel. The darker the roast, the more successful the substitution will be.

■■   HERBAL TEAS   ■■

WHAT TO USE INSTEAD

Fresh or dried herbs. Many herbs and spices make wonderful homemade alternatives to pricey store-bought herbal teas. For example, you can steep a teaball filled with one bay leaf, or three or four whole cloves, or a small piece of cinnamon stick, or ½ teaspoon dried sage leaves, or ½ teaspoon crushed mint leaves in a cup of boiling water for a few minutes. Then remove the teaball, sweeten the tea to taste, and serve.

If you are sensitive to any of these herbs or plants, of course you shouldn't use these teas.

Orange or lemon peel.   Peel a 2-inch strip of lemon or orange peel, twist the peel and steep it in a cup of boiling water. Sweeten to taste and serve.

Hot spiced apple juice.   Heat one cup apple juice. Add a pinch of cinnamon and a drop of lemon juice or vinegar. Or use a tablespoon of apple juice to sweeten a cup of regular orange pekoe tea.

■■   **TEA**   ■■

WHAT TO USE INSTEAD

Honey.   One or 2 teaspoons honey in a cup of boiling water is a surprisingly good caffeine-free alternative to ordinary tea sweetened with sugar. To substitute for an orange-flavored tea, add a twist of orange peel to the honey.

NOTES: YOUR OWN ALTERNATIVES

_____

_____

_____

_____

_____

_____

_____

_____

_____

_____

_____

_____

_____

_____

_____

_____

_____

_____

_____

_____

_____

_____

_____

_____

_____

_____

_____

_____

_____

_____

_____

_____

FOOD

BEANS, NUTS, RICE & SEEDS

RULE 1. When substituting one type
of bean or rice for another,
check the cooking time.
Some of these protein-rich
foods cook a lot faster than others,
which means you must adjust your recipe
to fit the new ingredients.
RULE 2. What looks like a
substitution may be not more than seman-
tics; lots of beans and nuts
have more than one name.
Chickpeas are also known as garbanzos,
navy beans are known as pea beans,
pine nuts are known as Indian nuts,
and peanuts are groundnuts.

▪▪   ALMONDS, GROUND   ▪▪

WHAT TO USE INSTEAD

Almond extract.   It lacks both the crunch and the texture, but ¼ teaspoon almond extract will give the flavor of a teaspoon of ground almonds.

▪▪   BEANS   ▪▪

WHAT TO USE INSTEAD

Canned beans.   One 1-pound can beans = ¾ cup raw dried beans = two cups cooked dried beans.

As a general rule, one cup raw dried beans = six cups when cooked.

▪▪   BROWN RICE   ▪▪

WHAT TO USE INSTEAD

Kasha.   It's a grain. It's brown. And it has a nutty flavor similar to the flavor of brown rice. When there's no brown rice in your cupboard, kasha is a more-than-acceptable substitute.

Kasha cooks in about ten minutes, as opposed to the 45 minutes it takes to cook brown rice—a plus when it comes to preparing the grain as a side dish, although it can complicate casserole cookery.

When substituting kasha for brown rice in a casserole or prepared dish, either cook the kasha first and mix it in at the end or adjust the cooking time to accommodate the kasha. Add it near the end, when everything else in the dish has cooked.

■■   COCONUT   ■■

WHAT TO USE INSTEAD

Dried coconut.   One tablespoon dried shreds or flakes soaked in water, squeezed dry = 1 ½ tablespoons shredded fresh coconut, soaked in water and squeezed dry.

A medium (1- to 1½-lb.) fresh coconut will yield four to five cups fresh shredded coconut meat.

■■   COCONUT MILK   ■■

WHAT TO USE INSTEAD

Whole milk.   In cooking, one cup whole milk = one cup coconut milk. As a substitute for coconut cream, use cream instead of milk.

■■   KIDNEY BEANS   ■■

WHAT TO USE INSTEAD

Great Northern beans, navy beans (pea beans), pinto beans.   All these white beans have a flavor and texture similar to that of kidney beans (which may be red or white). Like kidney beans, Great Northerns and navy beans cook in about an hour and a half. Pinto beans generally take half an hour more.

■■   NAVY BEANS   ■■

WHAT TO USE INSTEAD

Any small white beans.   This includes Great Northern, pea beans, and baby white lima beans.

■■　　　　　　PEANUT BUTTER　　　　　■■

WHAT TO USE INSTEAD

Ground, roasted peanuts.　To make ½ cup peanut butter: Place ⅔ cup roasted peanuts plus 2 teaspoons corn oil or peanut oil and ½ teaspoon salt (optional) in a blender or food processor, then blend or process until smooth.

■■　　　　　　PUMPKIN SEEDS　　　　　■■

WHAT TO USE INSTEAD

Hulled, oven-toasted seeds from an acorn squash or other winter squash.　Pumpkin is a variety of winter squash similar to acorn squash. To toast the edible seeds from a pumpkin or other winter squash, hull the seeds (take off their outer covering); spread the seeds on a cookie sheet; salt lightly and bake in the oven at 350° F for 15 minutes or until lightly brown. Use as a garnish or snack.

■■　　　　　TAHINA (TAHINI)　　　　　■■

WHAT TO USE INSTEAD

Peanut butter.　Tahina (or tahini) is a paste made of ground sesame seeds. It tastes like peanut butter, with a soft, oily texture that's more like "natural" peanut butters than ordinary commercial brands. Tahina is high in protein and fat; it has about 100 calories per tablespoon. Tahina is used in salad dressings and in Oriental cooking, particularly in sauces for noodle dishes. You can substitute an equal amount of smooth peanut butter; if the texture is too heavy, try adding a drop or two of peanut or sesame oil.

■■   WHITE RICE   ■■

WHAT TO USE INSTEAD

Brown rice, parboiled (converted) white rice, or pre-cooked (instant) white rice.   To make two cups cooked rice, start with ⅔ cup plain white rice, or ½ cup converted rice, or one cup instant rice, or ¾ cup brown rice, or ⅔ cup wild rice.

Ounce for ounce, brown rice has more riboflavin (vitamin B^2), niacin, phosphorus, potassium, and fat than white rices, while the white rices (which are fortified) have more calcium and iron.

■■   WILD RICE   ■■

WHAT TO USE INSTEAD

Brown rice alone or combine a mixture of brown rice and white rice.   Wild rice is not a rice; it's the seed of a wild grass. Because it is hard to gather and process, it is very expensive. As a result, it's usually sold mixed with white rice. To substitute a mixture of brown rice and white rice, prepare the rices separately (white rice cooks in about 10 - 15 minutes; brown rice can take as long as 45 minutes). Combine the cooked rices and serve.

Kasha.   Kasha's nutty flavor is not as sophisticated as the flavor of wild rice, but it is an acceptable and economical substitute.

NOTES: YOUR OWN ALTERNATIVES

_____

_____

CHEESE

It's nutritious
(2 tablespoons of cottage cheese have as
much protein as an ounce of meat).
It's delicious
(there are at least 700 known varieties).
And, it's literary
(when Marley's ghost appeared,
Scrooge blamed the whole thing
on the cheese he'd eaten for dinner).
Best of all, it substitutes.
You can make "cream cheese" without
cream, lasagne with a milk-free substitute
for ricotta, and whip up a cheese sauce
with no cheese at all.

■■　　　　　　　　　　BLUE　　　　　　　　　　■■

WHAT TO USE INSTEAD

Roquefort or Gorgonzola.   Blue cheese (spelled *blue* if it's made in America, and *bleu* if it's imported) is a mold-ripened cow's-milk cheese, originally from France. Roquefort is also a French mold-ripened cheese, but it's made from sheep's milk. Gorgonzola, a mold-ripened cheese similar in flavor to Roquefort and blue cheese, is Italian, made from either cow's or goat's milk. All three have a similar sharp distinctive flavor.

■■　　　　　　　　　　BRIE　　　　　　　　　　■■

WHAT TO USE INSTEAD

Camembert.   Brie comes in big wheels (or wedges) while Camembert comes in small ones, and Brie is usually more expensive, but both these soft-ripened cheeses have a smooth, buttery texture and a slightly pungent flavor that deepens as the cheese ripens, becoming softer and more aromatic.

■■　　　　　　　　CHEESE SAUCE　　　　　　　　■■

WHAT TO USE INSTEAD

Paprika.   No one will mistake this for the real thing, but when you're in a bind and there's absolutely no other way to cope, you may wish to try this cream sauce with a faint hint of American cheese flavor:

    1 tbsp. butter or margarine
    1½ tsp. paprika
    1 tbsp. flour

1 cup milk
½ tsp. salt
⅛ tsp. dry mustard (optional)

Melt the butter or margarine in a saucepan. Add the paprika and cook for a minute. Turn off the heat and blend in the flour. Add a little milk and blend in thoroughly. Then turn the heat on low and slowly add the rest of the milk, stirring constantly. Add salt and optional mustard powder.

■■   CREAM CHEESE   ■■

WHAT TO USE INSTEAD

Neufchatel cheese.   This creamy cheese has 74 calories and 6.7 grams of fat per ounce vs. 100 calories and 10 grams of fat in an ounce of cream cheese.

Drained yogurt.   Line a bowl or strainer with a square of cheesecloth. Pour 1 quart plain yogurt into the cheesecloth and pull up the corners of the square to make a bag. Tie the ends of the bag to one of the rods on a shelf in your refrigerator and put a bowl underneath to catch the whey that drains out of the yogurt. (Empty the bowl when necessary so that it doesn't overflow.) Let the yogurt drain for twenty-four hours. The result should be about 8 ounces of a thick, creamy, cheeselike substance you can substitute for cream cheese. This yogurt cheese has 30 calories and 1 gram of fat per ounce.

If your equipment isn't perfectly clean or if there is a stray mold in the refrigerator (from a fragrant, aged cheese, perhaps), the yogurt may turn moldy as it drains. Inspect it carefully before you use it and *discard it immediately if there is even the slightest hint of mold* (which may show up as a patch of color on the white yogurt).

Cottage cheese plus margarine.   To make a low-fat, low-cholesterol substitute for cream cheese, blend ½ cup low-fat cottage cheese with 2 tablespoons margarine until it is as smooth as you can get it (it's practically impossible to smooth out *all* the lumps). To make the cheese creamier, add a little low-fat or skim milk.

EDAM

WHAT TO USE INSTEAD

Gouda.   These Dutch cheeses (which may also be made in the United States) are virtual twins in flavor and texture.

GRUYÈRE

WHAT TO USE INSTEAD

Swiss cheese or Jarlsberg.   Either one will melt nicely as a substitute for gruyère in a fondue. Jarlsberg, a part-skim-milk cheese, has less fat per ounce than Swiss cheese.

PARMESAN

WHAT TO USE INSTEAD

Grated Romano.   Parmesan is made from skim milk, Romano is made from whole milk and has a more robust flavor, but they taste much the same when you dust them on pasta or stir them into a spaghetti sauce.

■■   RICOTTA   ■■

WHAT TO USE INSTEAD

Tofu (soybean curd).   Mash the tofu and use it as a milk-free, high-protein, low-calorie, low fat substitute for ricotta cheese in lasagne or in a stuffing for pasta shells.

Cottage cheese.   Put the cottage cheese through a blender, food processor, or strainer to smooth out the lumps (curds) and use it as a substitute for ricotta cheese in lasagne, in a stuffing for pasta shells or in a cheesecake.

■■   SWISS   ■■

WHAT TO USE INSTEAD

Jarlsberg cheese.   Jarlsberg looks and tastes like Swiss cheese but it is part skim milk, which means it has less fat and cholesterol per serving than Swiss.

NOTES: YOUR OWN ALTERNATIVES

_____

_____

_____

_____

_____

_____

_____

_____

_____

_____

_____

_____

_____

_____

_____

_____

_____

_____

_____

_____

_____

_____

_____

EGGS

You can't make an omelet
without breaking eggs,
but you can certainly make it
with less cholesterol and
fat than you are used to
by leaving out the yolks.
As for cakes and cookies,
you can make them
moist and tasty with
no eggs at all.

■■　　　　　BROWN EGGS　　　　　■■

WHAT TO USE INSTEAD

White eggs.　Nutritionally speaking, there's no difference at all between a brown egg and a white egg of the same size.

■■　　　　　EGG YOLKS　　　　　■■

WHAT TO USE INSTEAD

Egg whites.　An average egg yolk has 274 mg cholesterol; egg whites have no cholesterol at all. The following substitutions of whites for yolks may be useful for people who wish to reduce their intake of dietary cholesterol:

• **In scrambled or fried eggs:** Use one whole egg plus an egg white in place of two whole eggs.

• **In cakes:** Use two egg whites instead of two whole eggs. The cake will taste fine, but it won't be yellow.

• **In custards:** Use two egg whites in place of two whole eggs; add a little sugar or milk to keep the custard from becoming too firm.

Corn oil.　In pancakes or moist cookies: Substitute one egg white plus a tablespoon of corn oil for each whole egg.

■■　　　　　EGGS　　　　　■■

(A standard ["large"] egg weighs 2 ounces. One cup eggs = four "extra large" eggs, five "large" eggs, six "medium" eggs, or seven "small" eggs.)

WHAT TO USE INSTEAD

Dried egg powder.   Two and a half tablespoons sifted dried egg powder plus 2 ½ tablespoons water = one "large" egg.

Baking powder and water.   In cake baking, one teaspoon baking powder plus one tablespoon cool water will give you the leavening power of one egg and replace much of the liquid, but this substitute, which lacks the egg white's stabilizing proteins and egg yolk's texturizing fat, is far from perfect. It won't work in a delicate "sugar cake" or in a cake that requires several eggs. It works best in a cake whose recipe calls for about twice as much flour as sugar and no more than two eggs, such as a work-a-day "yellow cake".

Plain, unflavored gelatine.   As a general rule, one packet of unflavored gelatine dissolved in one cup of warm water can be used as a substitute for two eggs in a meat loaf or cheesecake. Here, for example, is Knox Gelatine's recipe for egg-free cheesecake:

"IT'S A SNAP" CHEESECAKE

1 envelope Knox Unflavored Gelatine
½ cup sugar
1 cup boiling water
2 packages (8 oz. ea.) cream cheese, softened
1 tsp. vanilla extract (optional)
9-inch graham-cracker crust

In a large bowl, mix gelatine with sugar; add boiling water, and stir until completely dissolved. With electric mixer, beat with cream cheese and vanilla until smooth. Pour into crust; chill until firm. Garnish, if desired, with fresh or canned fruit. Makes 8 servings.*

---

*Reprinted courtesy of Knox Gelatine, Inc.

NOTES: YOUR OWN ALTERNATIVES

_____

_____

_____

_____

_____

_____

_____

_____

_____

_____

_____

_____

_____

_____

_____

_____

_____

_____

_____

_____

_____

_____

FLOURS, THICKENERS, CRACKERS & CRUMBS

Flour is the binder holding
many a sturdy sauce together.
But not all flours
are equally necessary.
The one product for which
most people need a handy,
workable alternative is cake flour.
Every supermarket sells it. But do you
keep it in the house? Of course not. Most
of us measure out the "all-purpose"
and hope for the best.
There is a better way. It's listed here,
along with substitutes and alternatives for
other flours and thickeners.

■■   ALL - PURPOSE WHITE FLOUR   ■■

WHAT TO USE INSTEAD

Arrowroot, bread crumbs, cornstarch.   As a thickener, you can substitute 1 ½ teaspoons arrowroot, or 1 tablespoon fine bread crumbs, or 1 ½ teaspoons cornstarch for 1 tablespoon all-purpose white flour. In cookies you can substitute fine-ground unflavored bread crumbs for flour (in equal amounts).

Whole wheat flour.   In baking, you can use one cup fine-milled whole wheat flour, or one cup plus 2 tablespoons coarse-ground whole wheat flour, or 1¼ cups rye flour in place of one cup all-purpose white flour.

■■   ARROWROOT   ■■

WHAT TO USE INSTEAD

Cornstarch.   Like arrowroot, cornstarch thickens without clouding the sauce. Substitute 1 teaspoon cornstarch for 1 teaspoon arrowroot.

All-purpose white flour.   The flour will produce an opaque sauce rather than a clear one. Substitute 2 teaspoons flour for 1 teaspoon arrowroot.

■■   BAKING POWDERS   ■■

WHAT TO USE INSTEAD

Baking soda (sodium bicarbonate) plus cream of tartar.   One teaspoon baking powder = ½ teaspoon cream of tartar plus ⅓ teaspoon baking soda. One tablespoon baking powder = 1 teaspoon baking soda (sodium bicarbonate) plus 2 teaspoons cream of tartar. (These homemade alternatives can't be stored; they will lose their leavening power while standing.)

1½ teaspoons tartrate or phosphate baking powder ("single-acting") = 1 teaspoon "double-acting" baking powder.

In baking, one cup milk plus 2 teaspoons baking powder = one cup sour milk, buttermilk, yogurt, or sour cream plus ½ teaspoon baking soda (sodium bicarbonate).

■■ BAKING SODA ■■

WHAT TO USE INSTEAD

In baking, ½ teaspoon baking soda (sodium bicarbonate) plus one cup sour milk, buttermilk, yogurt, or sour cream = 2 teaspoons baking powder plus one cup milk.

■■ BREAD CRUMBS ■■

WHAT TO USE INSTEAD

White bread toasted in the oven until it is completely dried and then crumbled.

Corn flakes or plain bran cereal.   Crush the cereals and use them instead of bread crumbs as a sweet, crunchy coating on fish or chicken croquettes. The bran flakes are high in fiber, but both corn flakes and bran cereals are high in sugar.

Cracker crumbs.   Three-fourths cup cracker crumbs = one cup dry bread crumbs. If you use cracker crumbs instead of unflavored bread crumbs, always check the seasoning. Crackers, which are usually much saltier than bread crumbs, can change the flavor of your recipe. (Crackers also contain more fat.)

French bread.   Let the bread sit uncovered. Because it is made without fat, it will stale within hours and can be crushed into crumbs.

Grated raw potatoes.   Grated raw potatoes can be used instead of bread crumbs in meatballs or a meat loaf. The potatoes, which are low in fat, will keep the meat firm and moist. Grate one medium potato for each 1 ½ to 2 pounds ground meat. Then put the grated potato into a strainer and press down to squeeze out as much moisture as possible. (If you use the potatoes without squeezing out the moisture, your meat loaf or meatballs will be soggy.)

Melba toast (unflavored).   Crush the toast and use the crumbs. The flavored varieties are also useful as a substitute for similarly flavored bread crumbs.

■■　　　　　　**CAKE FLOUR**　　　　　　■■

WHAT TO USE INSTEAD

All-purpose white flour.   Cake flour is a finer grind than all-purpose flour. One cup cake flour = one cup minus 2 tablespoons all-purpose flour, sifted.

■■　　　　　　**CORNSTARCH**　　　　　　■■

WHAT TO USE INSTEAD

All-purpose white flour or quick-cooking tapioca.   As a thickener, 2 teaspoons all-purpose white flour or 4 teaspoons quick-cooking tapioca = 1 teaspoon cornstarch. Cornstarch makes a clear sauce; white flour and tapioca make an opaque sauce.

■■   CRACKER CRUMBS   ■■

WHAT TO USE INSTEAD

Bread crumbs. One cup bread crumbs = ¾ cup cracker crumbs. Because bread crumbs are less salty than cracker crumbs (or, in the case of graham cracker crumbs, much less sweet), you may have to correct the seasoning when you use these substitutes.

■■   CROUTONS   ■■

WHAT TO USE INSTEAD

Oven-toasted white bread. Butter both sides of a slice of white bread, trim the crust, cut the bread into cubes and toast the cubes in a medium (375º F) oven until browned. To make low-fat croutons, toast the bread without buttering it. For low-cholesterol croutons, use margarine instead of butter. For flavored croutons, add herbs or spices to the butter or margarine.

■■   FRENCH BREAD   ■■

WHAT TO USE INSTEAD

Italian bread. Italian bread and French bread are similar but not exactly the same. The long French loaf known as a *baguette* is made without any fat at all, while some long Italian breads have some. That's why Italian breads stay fresh for a day or two but French baguettes go stale practically while you're looking at them.

■■   SELF-RISING FLOUR   ■■

WHAT TO USE INSTEAD

All-purpose flour plus baking soda (sodium bicarbonate).
One cup self-rising flour = one cup all-purpose flour plus
1 ½ teaspoons baking powder and ½ teaspoon salt.

■■   TAPIOCA   ■■

WHAT TO USE INSTEAD

Cornstarch, all-purpose flour, or potato starch.   In thick-
ening power, ½ tablespoon cornstarch, or 1 tablespoon all-
purpose flour, or ½ tablespoon potato starch is equal to 1 tablespoon quick-cooking instant, granulated tapioca.

■■   WATER-CHESTNUT FLOUR   ■■

WHAT TO USE INSTEAD

Arrowroot, cornstarch.   Water chestnut powder, available
in gourmet and specialty food stores, is the thickener that
gives a lustrous gloss to Oriental sauces. As a thickener, 1
teaspoon arrowroot or 1 teaspoon cornstarch = 1 teaspoon
water chestnut powder, but neither produces the same shiny
finish.

■■   WHEAT FLOURS   ■■

WHAT TO USE INSTEAD

*Cornstarch, oatmeal, potato flour, rice flour, rye flour, soy
flour.*   As a substitute for one cup all-purpose white flour,
use: ½ cup cornstarch plus ½ cup potato flour or ½ cup

rice flour, plus 2 teaspoons baking powder for each cup of the cornstarch/flour mixture.

These substitutes are meant primarily for people who are allergic to wheat flours, and can be used in cookies, quick breads (breads made with baking soda or baking powder), pancakes, and waffles. They won't work in yeast breads, and if you want to use them in a cake, you may have to alter the recipe to compensate for the differences in how these flours perform. The easiest way to cope is to invest in a cookbook that has a collection of recipes for special diet needs. (See *Sources,* page 186).

■ ■ WHOLE WHEAT FLOUR ■ ■

WHAT TO USE INSTEAD

All-purpose white flour plus wheat germ or bran. For making bread, use ⅔ cup all-purpose white flour plus ⅓ cup powdered wheat germ or ¼ cup crushed bran cereal (without fruit) instead of one cup whole wheat flour. If you use bran cereal, reduce the sugar in the recipe by a tablespoon.

■ ■ YEAST ■ ■

WHAT TO USE INSTEAD

One cake yeast = one packet (2 teaspoons) active dry yeast. Cake yeast begins to work at temperatures between 50° and 80° F; active dry yeast at 105° to 115° F.

DO NOT use brewer's yeast, which has no leavening power at all.

NOTES: YOUR OWN ALTERNATIVES

_____

_____

_____

_____

_____

_____

_____

_____

_____

_____

_____

_____

_____

_____

_____

_____

_____

_____

_____

FRUIT

A rose is a rose is a rose,
but a cracker can stand in
for an apple;
a raisin is a reasonable
substitute for
several other dark,
sweet dried fruits;
and a cantaloupe can substitute
for practically everything orange
(except, of course,
an orange).

■■   APPLES (IN A PIE)   ■■

WHAT TO USE INSTEAD

Ritz crackers.   They are the basis for Nabisco Brands' classic Mock Apple Pie:

MOCK APPLE PIE

Pastry for two crust 9-inch pie
36 Ritz Crackers
2 cups water
2 cups sugar
2 teaspoons cream of tartar
2 tablespoons lemon juice
Grated rind of one lemon
Butter or margarine
Cinnamon

Roll out bottom crust of pastry and fit into 9-inch pie plate. Break Ritz Crackers coarsely into pastry-lined plate. Combine water, sugar, cream of tartar in saucepan; boil gently for 15 minutes. Add lemon juice and rind. Cool. Pour syrup over crackers, dot generously with butter or margarine, and sprinkle with cinnamon. Cover with top crust. Trim and flute edges together. Cut slits in top crust to let steam escape. Bake in a hot oven (425° F) 30 to 35 minutes, until crust is crisp and golden. Serve warm. Cut into 6 to 8 slices.*

■■   CURRANTS (DRIED)   ■■

WHAT TO USE INSTEAD

Raisins.   True currants are small berries; what most of us

---

*Reprinted by permission of Nabisco Brands, Inc.

call dried currants are actually dried white grapes, for which raisins are a satisfactory substitute.

■■   DATES   ■■

WHAT TO USE INSTEAD

Chopped seedless raisins or pitted prunes.   In baking, one cup chopped seedless raisins or pitted prunes = one cup chopped pitted dates.

■■   LEMON JUICE   ■■

WHAT TO USE INSTEAD

Distilled white vinegar.   You can use vinegar instead of lemon juice in fruit pies (particulárly apple pie), and hot tea (especially with sugar or honey). You can also sprinkle distilled white vinegar instead of lemon juice on peeled or sliced fresh-cut fruits and vegetables to keep them from darkening. As a general rule, ¼ teaspoon vinegar = 1 teaspoon lemon juice, or to taste.

Yogurt.   This is for cheesecakes. Use one cup drained, unflavored yogurt in place of one cup sour cream or as a substitute for 8 ounces cream cheese in a cream cheese cake. You'll get a lemony flavor even without using any lemon juice. (If you use the drained yogurt in place of cream cheese, don't substitute for more than one-third of the cream cheese. If you do, the result may be a stringy custard, not a creamy cake. A method for draining yogurt appears on page 111.

Vitamin C tablets.   To keep fresh vegetables and fruits from darkening when peeled or sliced, dissolve 500 mg Vita-

min C in two cups of water and brush the solution over the
cut surfaces of the fruit or vegetables.

■■　　　　　　　　**LEMON PEEL**　　　　　　　　■■

WHAT TO USE INSTEAD

Lemon juice or lemon extract.　　Two tablespoons fresh lemon juice or ½ teaspoon lemon extract = 1 teaspoon fresh-
grated lemon peel (zest).

■■　　　　　　**MANDARIN ORANGES**　　　　　　■■

WHAT TO USE INSTEAD

Tangerines.　　Section the tangerines, remove the seeds, and
use the sections to brighten up a salad. (Canned "Mandarin
oranges" are actually blanched tangerines.)

■■　　　　　　　　**MANGOES**　　　　　　　　■■

WHAT TO USE INSTEAD

Cantaloupe, papaya.　　Slice and use in place of mangoes in
fruit salad or recipes for chutneys.

■■　　　　　　　　**PAPAYA**　　　　　　　　■■

WHAT TO USE INSTEAD

Cantaloupe, mangoes.　　Sliced, in a salad, both look like pa-
payas, but mangoes are closer in texture and taste.

■■ PRUNES ■■

WHAT TO USE INSTEAD

Seedless raisins. In recipes for purées to be used in baking (prune Danish, fruit soufflé), a cup of seedless raisins will serve as a substitute for a cup of chopped pitted prunes.

■■ RAISINS ■■

WHAT TO USE INSTEAD

Chopped pitted prunes. One cup chopped prunes is the equivalent of one cup seedless raisins.

NOTES: YOUR OWN ALTERNATIVES

_____

_____

_____

_____

_____

_____

_____

_____

_____

_____

MEAT, FISH & POULTRY

There's no true substitute
for sirloin steak,
but hamburger
is fair game.
So is pâté de fois gras
and fish of every stripe.
And there's a new fin-fish
substitute for shellfish
that some food chemists
predict may soon
substitute for pasta, meat,
and snack foods, too.

■■　　　　　　　　CAVIAR　　　　　　　　■■

WHAT TO USE INSTEAD

Lumpfish or salmon roe. 　True caviar is the roe (eggs) of the sturgeon. The "best" is the shiny, translucent grains from the Iranian (Beluga) sturgeon or from sturgeon of the Caspian Sea (Sevruga). Lumpfish roe (which is black) and salmon roe (which is orange-pink) are saltier and more gelatinous than sturgeon roe. Also a *lot* less expensive.

Seasoned chopped eggplant. 　Cook a medium whole eggplant in boiling water until the eggplant is tender. Take the eggplant out of the water, let it cool, peel it, and chop it fine. Sauté the chopped eggplant in 2 to 3 tablespoons olive oil with ½ cup chopped onion, one small peeled chopped tomato (or one tablespoon tomato juice), and 2 teaspoons lemon juice or vinegar. When most of the liquid has evaporated from the eggplant mixture, add salt and pepper to taste. Remove the mixture from the heat, chill it thoroughly for several hours in the refrigerator, and serve ice-cold with crackers as a relatively inexpensive vegetarian substitute for caviar.

■■　　　　　　　　　FISH　　　　　　　　　■■

WHAT TO USE INSTEAD

A fish's fat content affects its flavor and determines how it can be cooked. 　The following groups of fish are similar in fat content and, although they may have slightly different tastes, they can often be substituted for one another.

● **Lean fish:** Cod, grouper, hake, halibut (Atlantic, California, Pacific), ocean perch, pike, skate, tilefish

● **Moderately fatty fish:** Bass, bluefish, catfish, porgy, swordfish, tuna, yellowtail

• **Fatty fish:** Bonito, butterfish, halibut (Greenland), mackerel, pompano, salmon, trout

■■   GROUND BEEF OR PORK   ■■

WHAT TO USE INSTEAD

Ground turkey.   This is a versatile, low-fat substitute for ground beef and pork. Like pork, it must be thoroughly cooked, past the pink stage, so it works best in meat loaf and meatballs. It's also a great substitute for the ground-pork filling in Chinese dumplings; you can use small meatballs of ground turkey as a substitute for pork chunks in most Oriental recipes.

■■   PÂTÉ DE FOIS GRAS   ■■

WHAT TO USE INSTEAD

Chopped chicken liver.   To match the suave, smooth flavor and texture of the ground goose livers used in true pâté de fois gras, sauté the chicken livers, then grind them very smooth and season with salt, pepper, and brandy or cream sherry to taste.

■■   PROSCIUTTO   ■■

WHAT TO USE INSTEAD

Virginia ham.   Slice the Virginia ham paper thin and serve it over melon (cantaloupe, casaba, or honeydew). The sweet, smoky flavor of the Virginia ham is not as subtle and spicy as prosciutto's, but it's an acceptable alternative.

■■ SHELLFISH ■■

WHAT TO USE INSTEAD

Surimi. Surimi is real fish (usually Pacific whitefish), cleaned, chopped, rinsed and strained into a paste that is mixed with sugar, sorbitol, and other additives such as monosodium glutamate, (MSG), starch, and salt. Surimi tastes likes shellfish and can be molded and dyed to look like real crabmeat, lobster, shrimp, and scallops. It is a high-protein, low-fat food, and—because it is made from a fin fish—has less cholesterol than real shellfish. On the other hand, added salt and MSG make it higher in sodium.

■■ SWEETBREADS ■■

WHAT TO USE INSTEAD

Brains. The texture of brains is similar to that of sweetbreads (thymus glands from a calf or a cow). Both organ foods have a bland flavor that works best when the brains or sweetbreads are simmered, then chilled, and finally seasoned and sautéed or pan-fried in a delicate coating.

■■ TUNA (CANNED) ■■

WHAT TO USE INSTEAD

Canned mackerel. The flavor of canned mackerel is stronger than that of canned white-meat tuna, but you can mix them half-and-half to stretch the more expensive tuna. Or you can use the mackerel instead of dark tuna in croquettes or tuna-noodle casseroles.

■■   **VEAL SCALOPPINE**   ■■

WHAT TO USE INSTEAD

Turkey fillets or ground turkey.   When veal scalloppine costs more than $10 a pound, turkey breast sliced into fillets or ground turkey pressed into patties are a thoroughly sensible substitute. They are both economical but you may have to add some extra seasoning to compensate for turkey's blander flavor.

Thin-sliced eggplant.   This low-fat, no-cholesterol, vegetarian alternative is a more-than-acceptable substitute in Italian cookery.

NOTES: YOUR OWN ALTERNATIVES

_____

_____

_____

_____

_____

_____

_____

_____

_____

_____

_____

_____

_____

_____

_____

_____

_____

_____

_____

_____

_____

_____

_____

_____

_____

_____

_____

_____

_____

_____

_____

_____

MILK, BUTTER & CREAM

The good news is
calcium and protein.
The bad news is cholesterol and fat.
It takes some truly
fancy dancing around the dairy case
to get the former without the latter,
but that doesn't mean
it can't be done.
Given the right alternatives,
you can make whipped cream
without cream,
butter cake without butter,
and a milk substitute
that never saw a cow.

■■   BUTTER   ■■

WHAT TO USE INSTEAD

Margarine, lard, or vegetable oil.   One tablespoon butter
= 1 tablespoon margarine or ¾ tablespoon vegetable oil or
¾ tablespoon lard. One cup butter = one cup margarine or
⅞ cup vegetable oil or ⅞ cup lard. One cup melted butter =
one cup oil.

Salt.   If you are out of butter or oil, you can keep pancakes
from sticking to an iron griddle or an uncoated frying pan by
sprinkling lots of salt into the cold pan. Rub the salt into the
pan with a paper towel. Pour off salt, heat pan and proceed
as usual, taking care to turn the pancakes as soon as there
are bubbles all over the top surface (including the center).

■■   BUTTERMILK   ■■

WHAT TO USE INSTEAD

*Fresh whole, low-fat milk or skim milk plus lemon juice or
distilled white vinegar or cream of tartar.*   As a substitute
for one cup buttermilk in cooking: Put 1 tablespoon of lemon
juice or distilled white vinegar or 1¼ tablespoons cream of
tartar in an 8-ounce measuring cup and add enough milk to
fill the cup. Let the milk stand for a few minutes until it
thickens.

Whole milk plus baking powder.   In cakes or pancakes,
you can substitute one cup whole milk plus 2 teaspoons baking powder for one cup buttermilk plus ½ teaspoon baking
soda.

Yogurt.   In cooking or baking or simply for eating, one cup
low-fat yogurt = one cup buttermilk.

■ ■   CREAM SAUCE   ■ ■

WHAT TO USE INSTEAD

Dried milk, margarine, and flour.   This will make a rich-tasting but reduced-fat, low-cholesterol substitute:

REDUCED FAT, LOW-CHOLESTEROL CREAM SAUCE

1 tbsp. margarine
1 tbsp. all-purpose white flour
1 cup plus 2 tbsp. low-fat milk
  or reconstituted low-fat dry milk

Melt margarine in saucepan. Remove from heat. Blend in flour. Add 2 tablespoons milk and stir to blend. Return the pot to the heat, keep the flame low, and add the rest of the milk, stirring constantly. Salt to taste.

■ ■   CRÈME FRAÎCHE   ■ ■

WHAT TO USE INSTEAD

Heavy, (whipping) cream plus cultured buttermilk or yogurt with active bacteria.   *Crème fraîche* is a cultured milk that has the consistency of sour cream but tastes sweet. To make this substitute, add 1 teaspoon cultured buttermilk or yogurt with live bacteria to a cup of heavy cream. Then let the cream stand at room temperature until it thickens. Refrigerate and use as soon as possible.

■ ■   MARGARINE   ■ ■

WHAT TO USE INSTEAD

Butter or corn oil.   In baking, one cup butter or ¾ cup corn oil = one cup margarine.

■■   MILK   ■■

WHAT TO USE INSTEAD

Skim milk or nonfat powdered milk.   In cooking, one cup
skim milk or one cup reconstituted nonfat dry milk plus 2
teaspoons butter or margarine or corn oil = one cup whole
milk. To reduce a recipe's fat and/or cholesterol content, use
plain skim milk or reconstituted nonfat dry milk (no butter,
margarine, or corn oil) in place of whole milk.

Evaporated milk.   Half a cup of evaporated milk plus ½
cup water = one cup whole milk.

Soy milk.   One cup soy milk = one cup whole milk.

Tofu.   In salad dressing, dips, and cream soups, one cup
puréed tofu = one cup milk.

■■   SOUR CREAM   ■■

WHAT TO USE INSTEAD

Plain, unflavored yogurt.   When baking cakes or bread,
you can substitute one cup plain yogurt for one cup sour
cream. For dips, it's best to drain the yogurt until it is as
thick as sour cream. A method for draining yogurt appears
on page 111.

Buttermilk.   For cake or bread recipes, one cup buttermilk
= one cup sour cream.

Cottage cheese plus lemon juice and skimmed milk.   To
make one cup reduced-fat, lower-calorie imitation sour
cream, add 1 tablespoon lemon juice to a cup of cottage
cheese. Add buttermilk or skim milk as required and beat
until smooth.

Evaporated milk or sweet cream plus lemon juice or

vinegar.   For sauces or salad dressing, add 1 teaspoon of lemon juice or vinegar to each cup of milk or cream, let the liquid sit until slightly thickened, and use as required. One cup of this mixture = one cup sour cream.

■ ■   **SWEET CREAM**   ■ ■

WHAT TO USE INSTEAD

Milk plus butter or margarine.   In cooking, ¾ cup whole milk plus ⅓ cup unsalted butter or margarine = one cup heavy sweet cream. To "lighten" the cream, reduce the amount of fat: ¾ cup whole milk plus ¼ cup unsalted butter or margarine = one cup light cream.

Evaporated milk.   One cup undiluted evaporated milk = one cup sweet cream.

These substitutes cannot be whipped.

■ ■   **WHIPPING CREAM**   ■ ■

WHAT TO USE INSTEAD

Evaporated milk.   Prepare in one of the following ways:

• Chill the can of milk for at least 12 hours. Then open the can and pour the milk into a clean bowl, add 1 ½ tablespoons lemon juice and ½ teaspoon vanilla for each 6 ounces of milk, and whip the mixture until it is stiff and fluffy. Sweeten to taste.

• Pour 10 oz. (1 large or 2 small cans) of evaporated milk into a freezer tray and let sit in freezer until milk is slushy. DO NOT LET IT FREEZE SOLID. Then pour the milk into a chilled bowl and whip until it stands in peaks. Add vanilla and sweeten to taste.

Nonfat dry milk. Dissolve ½ cup powdered milk in ⅓ - ½ cup cold water, chill in the refrigerator for at least an hour, and whip until it stiffens. When the mixture is stiff, add vanilla and whip again. Sweeten to taste.

Drained vanilla yogurt. Some may find this an acceptable substitute for whipped cream. A method to drain yogurt appears on page 111. To make your own vanilla yogurt topping, drain plain yogurt as directed, then add vanilla extract and granulated white sugar to taste. You may be surprised to see how much sugar it takes to sweeten the yogurt.

■■ **YOGURT** ■■

WHAT TO USE INSTEAD

Buttermilk. In baking, one cup buttermilk = one cup plain yogurt.

Fresh milk plus lemon juice or distilled white vinegar. Add 1 teaspoon lemon juice or distilled white vinegar to one cup whole or skim milk, and let the milk stand until it thickens. In baking, one cup of this thickened milk = one cup yogurt.

Sour cream. In baking, one cup sour cream = one cup yogurt. The sour cream is higher in fat.

NOTES: YOUR OWN ALTERNATIVES

_____

_____

_____

_____

SUGARS & SWEETS

Why do sweet foods
make so many people angry?
"Empty calories," "fake food,"
"junk food"—you know the litany.
But what about "energy"?
What about "good taste"?
What about "I like it"?
Listen, the next time someone
starts in on your favorite treats,
whisper this one in his ear:
"Nature must *love* sweet foods.
She made so many of them."
That ought to clear the air
just long enough for you to
grab a chocolate bonbon.

■■   BAKING CHOCOLATE   ■■

WHAT TO USE INSTEAD

Cocoa powder.   Three tablespoons plain cocoa powder plus one tablespoon butter, margarine, or corn oil = 1 ounce baking chocolate. To reduce the fat content, substitute 1 tablespoon water for the butter, margarine, or corn oil.

Carob powder.   Three tablespoons carob flour plus 2 tablespoons liquid equal 1 ounce unsweetened baking chocolate. This substitute is sweeter than baking chocolate since carob contains more natural sugars than cocoa.

■■   CHOCOLATE FUDGE SAUCE   ■■

WHAT TO USE INSTEAD

Plain cocoa powder plus sugar and water.   Combine 2 tablespoons plain cocoa powder, 2 tablespoons sugar, and 1 tablespoon water in a double boiler and stir to mix thoroughly. Cook over a very low flame, stirring constantly until the cocoa and sugar have melted completely. Yield: 3 tablespoons sauce. (The recipe may be doubled as needed.) Pour the sauce over ice cream or pound cake; it will harden into a fudgy topping.

■■   CONFECTIONER'S SUGAR   ■■

WHAT TO USE INSTEAD

Granulated sugar.   Confectioner's sugar (powdered sugar) is a finer version of regular granulated sugar. To make an acceptable substitute, process granulated sugar in your blender and add a dash of cornstarch to keep the fine sugar from caking.

■■ HONEY ■■

WHAT TO USE INSTEAD

Brown sugar, corn syrup, white sugar. In baking, you can use one of the following as a substitute for one cup honey: 1 ½ cups brown sugar plus ¼ cup water, one cup corn syrup, or 1¼ cups table sugar plus ¼ cup water.

■■ MAPLE SUGAR ■■

WHAT TO USE INSTEAD

Granulated white sugar (table sugar). Half a cup white sugar = the sweetening power of ¼ cup maple sugar.

Maple syrup. In baking, ½ cup maple syrup = ⅔ cup maple sugar. Reduce the amount of liquid in the recipe by 1 ½ tablespoons for every half cup of syrup you use as a substitute for the sugar.

■■ WHITE SUGAR (TABLE SUGAR) ■■

WHAT TO USE INSTEAD

Brown sugar, corn syrup, honey, or molasses. In baking, you can use one of the following in place of one cup white sugar: one cup firmly packed brown sugar, 1 ⅓ cups granulated brown sugar, ¾ cup honey (eliminate ¼ cup liquid from your recipe), or 1 ⅓ cup molasses (eliminate ¼ cup liquid from your recipe).

Apple juice concentrate. To "proof" yeast for making bread, you can substitute 1 teaspoon apple juice concentrate for 1 tablespoon.

NOTES: YOUR OWN ALTERNATIVES

_____

_____

_____

_____

_____

_____

_____

_____

_____

_____

_____

_____

_____

_____

_____

_____

_____

_____

_____

_____

_____

_____

VEGETABLES

The key to
substituting one vegetable
successfully for another,
is to capitalize
on close relationships.
Most roots will sweeten
your soups and stews
(even if they come
in different colors and textures).
Most yellow winter squashes
are interchangeable;
so are the green
and yellow summer ones.
And, depending on your recipe,
a tomato sauce may
be as good as a tomato.

■■ BUTTERHEAD LETTUCE ■■

WHAT TO USE INSTEAD

Loose-leaf lettuce. Butterhead is the family name for Bibb and Boston lettuces, whose delicate flavor and texture are similar to those of green and red loose-leaf lettuces.

■■ CABBAGE ■■

WHAT TO USE INSTEAD

Bibb, Boston, iceberg or romaine lettuce leaves. As a substitute for green cabbage in a recipe for stuffed cabbage: Immerse the lettuce leaves in boiling water for a few minutes until they are pliable enough to fold around the stuffing. Then prepare as your recipe directs.

■■ CARROTS ■■

WHAT TO USE INSTEAD

In soups or stews: parsnips, white turnips. The color and texture are different but each will add sweetness to the dish.

■■ CHICORY ■■

WHAT TO USE INSTEAD

Curly endive or escarole. Both have a slightly bitter taste and a crunchy texture similar to chicory's.

Arugula or fresh spinach. These add a slightly bitter flavor to your salad, but they aren't crunchy.

■■   CUCUMBER   ■■

WHAT TO USE INSTEAD

Zucchini or yellow summer squash. Slice the squash (without or without the peel) and use in place of cucumber slices in salads or as a garnish.

■■   ESCAROLE   ■■

WHAT TO USE INSTEAD

Chicory, arugula, or spinach. Each will add a similar bitter flavor to salad. They're all deep-green leaves, good sources of the vitamin A-precursor, betacarotene.

■■   LEEKS   ■■

WHAT TO USE INSTEAD

Green onions (scallions). Scallions have a sharper, more distinctive flavor than leeks, but they'll do nicely in a pinch.

■■   MUSHROOMS   ■■

WHAT TO USE INSTEAD

Canned mushrooms or dried mushrooms. As a general rule, 3 ounces dried mushrooms or 8 ounces canned mushrooms (drained weight, 6-7 oz.) = 1 pound fresh mushrooms.

NOTE: Different mushrooms have different flavors, some more intense than others. For example, the flavor of large black dried mushrooms is much deeper and richer than the flavor of small fresh white button mushrooms. If you want to substitute one for the other, you'll have to experiment with quantities to get exactly the taste you're looking for.

■■   **OLIVE OIL**   ■■

WHAT TO USE INSTEAD

Corn oil flavored with green olives.   Steep the olives in the oil for at least two days, then use the oil in salad dressings.

■■   **ONIONS**   ■■

WHAT TO USE INSTEAD

Onion powder or minced dried onion.   In cooking, 1 teaspoon onion powder or 1 tablespoon minced dried onion equals the flavor of one small, fresh, yellow onion.

■■   **PARSNIPS**   ■■

WHAT TO USE INSTEAD

Carrots or white turnips.   The textures and colors vary, but either of these root vegetables will sweeten a soup or stew. And you can also serve them as a side dish.

■■   **POTATOES**   ■■

WHAT TO USE INSTEAD

Small white turnips.   This is an alternative that looks the same even though it tastes entirely different. Peeled white turnips resemble peeled white potatoes, especially if you dust them with paprika and roast them along with beef, pork, or poultry. They are much lower in calories.

■■ PUMPKIN ■■

WHAT TO USE INSTEAD

Any yellow winter squash.   Pumpkin is a winter squash, whose flavor is so similar to the flavor of other yellow winter squashes that the USDA permits other winter squashes to be packed in with the pumpkin in cans labeled pumpkin. You can use these squashes as a substitute for pumpkin in soups, pies,and as a side dish.

■ RED OR YELLOW ■
■ SWEET BELL PEPPERS ■

WHAT TO USE INSTEAD

Green bell peppers.   Despite the price difference (yellow and red peppers may cost three times more than green ones) and the difference in color, these are all the same vegetable in different stages of ripeness. Both the green and the yellow ones may turn red when they mature.

■■ SHALLOTS ■■

WHAT TO USE INSTEAD

Scallions (green onions).   The small white bulbs are less intensely flavored than shallots but are useful substitutes in a pinch.

Small yellow or white onions.   Deepen the flavor with a pinch of garlic or a little sugar and you'll have a good, if not absolutely perfect, alternative.

■■   SNOW PEA PODS   ■■

WHAT TO USE INSTEAD

Sugar pea pods.   The peas in these pods develop more fully than the peas in snow pea pods, but the pods are completely edible.

Fresh green peas, sliced green peppers, or green beans sliced on the diagonal.   When snow pea pods are unavailable, these substitutes will add a green flavor and attractive color to Oriental dishes.

■■   TOMATOES   ■■

WHAT TO USE INSTEAD

Canned tomatoes.   One cup canned tomatoes = 1⅓ cups quartered fresh tomatoes.

Tomato sauce.   Four ounces tomato sauce plus 4 ounces water equals the flavor of one cup stewed or canned tomatoes.

■■   WHITE TURNIPS   ■■

WHAT TO USE INSTEAD

Parsnips.   Prepare the same way you would prepare white turnips.

NOTES: YOUR OWN ALTERNATIVES

_____

_____

_____

_____

_____

_____

_____

_____

_____

_____

_____

_____

_____

_____

_____

_____

_____

_____

_____

_____

_____

_____

_____

VITAMINS & MINERALS

Those of us who
like to get our vitamins
from food, not pills,
know all about the "good stuff."
For vitamin C,
we squeeze an orange.
For protein,
we broil some lean beef.
For calcium, we pour the milk.
But what if you're sensitive
to citrus or on a vegetarian diet
or unable to digest milk?
Here's a list of alternate foods,
just as good as the good stuff.*

---

*(Note: The figures here come from the Department of Agriculture's series of nutrient tables, *Composition of Foods*.)

■■   CALCIUM   ■■

Calcium protects bones and teeth. The best source is cheddar cheese which, ounce for ounce, has six times the calcium in milk. But milk is more versatile and easier to incorporate into your diet, which makes it the all-around best source. Three 8-ounce glasses of whole, lowfat or skim milk provide 873-906 mg calcium, about 110 percent of the RDA for a healthy adult.

WHAT TO USE INSTEAD

The following amounts of specific foods have approximately the same amount of calcium as one glass of milk.

Dairy foods:

   1 ⅓ ounces cheddar cheese
   2 ounces blue cheese
   13 ounces cream cheese
   2 ounces whole milk mozzarella
   1 ½ ounces part skim milk mozzarella
   ⅔ cup whole milk ricotta cheese
   ½ cup part skim milk ricotta
   1 cup sour cream
   1 ¾ cups vanilla ice cream
   10 whole eggs

Seafood:

   15 ounces fresh clams (meat only)
   17-24 fresh oysters (meat only)
   5 ounces canned salmon (with bones)
   2 ⅓ ounces drained sardines (with bones)
   9 ounces drained, canned shrimp
   3 pounds drained canned solid white tuna (water-pack)

Fruit:

   29 medium apples

138 large dried apricot halves
50 whole pitted dates
6 medium oranges

Grains:

10 3½-inch bagels
10-20 slices commercial bread made without added
   calcium
15 cups regular oatmeal

Meat & poultry:

6 pounds broiled lean hamburger patty
4 pounds roast white meat chicken

Vegetables:

6 steamed globe artichokes
3½ cups drained, cooked Great Northern or navy beans
6 cups cooked black, kidney or lima beans
2½ cups cooked drained soybeans
3 pieces (2.5 x 2.75 x 1″) soybean curd
2 spears fresh broccoli
2 cups steamed, drained fresh dandelion greens
3 cups steamed, drained fresh kale
3 6-inch heads of iceberg lettuce
1 cup steamed, drained fresh spinach
5 cups canned tomatoes (with liquid)
1½ cups steamed drained fresh turnip greens

■■   **IRON**   ■■

Iron, which is an important constituent of hemoglobin, makes it possible for our blood to carry oxygen around our bodies. The most common sign of iron deficiency is an anemia that reduces the level of oxygen in our tissues, making us pale, tired, cold, and weak.

WHAT TO USE INSTEAD

The following portions of food will provide approximately the same amount of iron as one 3.5-ounce (100 gram) serving of braised beef liver which has 6.8 mg iron, one-third the RDA for a healthy adult woman.

Dairy products:

    7 whole eggs
    7 cups grated parmesan cheese
    100 cups whole milk

Seafood:

    8 ounces fresh clams (meat only)
    6-8 fresh oysters (meat only)
    2 pounds canned salmon (with liquid)
    8 ounces drained, canned sardines
    15 ounces drained, canned shrimp
    2 pounds drained, canned (water pack) solid white meat
        tuna

Grain products:

    7 slices French bread
    10 slices enriched oatmeal, rye or white bread
    8 slices enriched whole wheat or pumpernickel bread
    4⅓ cups regular oatmeal
    34 cups air-popped popcorn
    7 cups cooked brown rice
    3⅘ cups cooked enriched white rice
    3½ cups cooked spaghetti
    1¼ cups all-purpose white flour (enriched) or whole
        wheat flour

Meat:

    7 ounces lean braised beef
    10 ounces broiled hamburger

7 ounces lean broiled sirloin steak

12 ounces lean roast leg of lamb

69 medium slices cooked bacon or 34 "brown and serve" link sausages

1 ½ pounds lean, fried pork chop or roast white meat chicken

1 ½ pounds braised veal cutlet

Nuts & seeds:

7 ounces mixed (dry-roast) nuts

1 ½ ounces dry, hulled pumpkin seeds

10 tablespoons tahini (ground sesame seeds)

■■   VITAMIN A   ■■

Vitamin A protects our sight and all the tissues of our bodies. In addition, present research suggests that betacarotene, a precursor of Vitamin A found in orange, red and deep yellow vegetables, may offer some protection against cancers of the larynx, esophagus and lungs. Caution: Vitamin A may be toxic in amounts larger than the RDA.

WHAT TO USE INSTEAD

The following foods provide approximately 5,000 IU (international Units) of vitamin A, 100% of the RDA and the same amount as you would get in ½ ounce braised beef liver or ½ oz fresh raw carrots.

Dairy foods:

4 cups shredded cheddar cheese

31 cups lowfat cottage cheese

12 ½ ounces cream cheese

3 cups sour cream

16 cups whole milk

10 cups skim milk
9 cups vanilla ice cream
18 8-ounce containers whole milk yogurt
19 whole eggs

Fish & shellfish:

3 pounds baked red salmon

Fruit:

5 ½ fresh apricots
5 California avocados or 3 Florida avocados
¼ cantaloupe
2 ¾ cups canned (water pack) sour cherries
8 pink grapefruits
½ mango
5 fresh nectarines
10 ½ peaches
3 ½ cups cooked plantains
21 extra large prunes
6 ½ tangerines
3 (4 x 8 inch) pieces of watermelon

Vegetables:

3 ⅓ cups cooked drained fresh asparagus
2 spears fresh broccoli
4 ½ cups fresh cooked Brussels sprouts
7 cups shredded Savoy cabbage
29 ears fresh-cooked yellow corn
½ cup cooked fresh dandelion greens
6 cups cooked fresh greenbeans
3 heads iceberg lettuce (6″ diameter)
3 ⅘ cups drained canned peas
1 ounce canned pumpkin
⅕ baked sweet potato
3 ½ fresh tomatoes

■■ VITAMIN C ■■

Vitamin C helps to build and maintain connective tissues and the walls of our blood vessels. The Vitamin C-deficiency disease, scurvy, is characterized by bleeding and bruising. The vitamin also promotes healing and may protect against viruses, such as those that cause the common cold.

WHAT TO USE INSTEAD

The standard source of vitamin C is citrus fruit, particularly oranges, which provide about 15 mg Vitamin C per ounce. The following foods will give you about 124 mg vitamin C (two times the RDA for a healthy adult), the same amount you'd get from one cup of fresh-squeezed orange juice.

Dairy food:

   62 cups whole milk

Fish and shellfish:

   2.6 pounds fresh clams (meat only)
   5 cups fresh oysters (meat only)

Fruit:

   16 medium apples (with peel)
   34 fresh apricots
   6 ½ cups raw blueberries
   ½ cantaloupe
   1 ½ grapefruits
   1 ⅓ cups fresh grapefruit juice
   248 Thompson seedless grapes
   2 kiwi fruits
   2 mangoes
   21 medium peaches
   18 medium pears
   5 cups diced fresh pineapple

21 plums
248 extra large prunes
1 ½ cups fresh strawberries
5 tangerines

Vegetables:

14 artichokes, cooked and drained
2 ½ cups cooked, drained fresh asparagus
14 cups cooked drained fresh beets
1 spear fresh broccoli
1 ⅓ cups cooked fresh Brussels sprouts
3 ¾ cups shredded green cabbage
1 ¾ cups raw cauliflower florets
41 stalks fresh celery
6 ½ cups cooked drained dandelion greens
1 ⅓ cups cooked drained kohlrabi
8 cups drained canned peas
5 baked potatoes
3 ½ cups canned sauerkraut with liquid
4 ½ baked sweet potatoes
5 ½ fresh tomatoes

NOTES: YOUR OWN ALTERNATIVES

_____

_____

_____

_____

_____

_____

_____

_____

_____

_____

_____

_____

_____

_____

_____

_____

_____

_____

_____

_____

_____

_____

_____

_____

_____

_____

_____

_____

_____

SEASONINGS

CONDIMENTS & COOKING AIDS

These are the products
that make food taste better
with a minimum of fuss.
Everybody uses them;
no one with
a smidgen of pretension
to culinary creativity
will admit it.
Not make
your own mayonnaise?
Use catsup as a flavoring?
How *declassé*.
(And how convenient!)

■■ BEEF BROTH ■■

WHAT TO USE INSTEAD

Bouillon cube. One bouillon cube plus one cup of boiling water = one cup beef broth.

Beef extract (Bovril). One teaspoon beef extract plus one cup boiling water = one cup beef bouillon. (The beef extract can also be used to make pan gravy more intensely "beefy.")

■■ CATSUP ■■

WHAT TO USE INSTEAD

Tomato sauce plus sugar and vinegar. To substitute for one cup tomato catsup, add 2 ounces sugar and 1 tablespoon distilled white vinegar to 8 ounces plain tomato sauce. Mix and use immediately. Discard any leftover substitute catsup.

■■ CHINESE MUSTARD ■■

WHAT TO USE INSTEAD

Dry mustard powder mixed with just enough warm water to make a paste. For the strongest flavor, use the paste right away. The longer it sits, the less sharp it will be.

■■ COFFEE FILTERS ■■

WHAT TO USE INSTEAD

A clean linen handkerchief. While paper towels, paper napkins, and paper tissues sound like a reasonable substitutes for coffee filters, they may contain dyes or other chemicals that can spoil the taste of the coffee.

■■ COURT BOUILLON (FISH STOCK) ■■

WHAT TO USE INSTEAD

Bottled clam juice or the liquid from water-pack canned fish (tuna, salmon, shrimp, or clams—plain, not smoked).   Season the liquid to taste with herbs (parsley, thyme), spices (pepper), and dry white wine or vermouth. Don't add salt without tasting the liquid first: some canned fish is already very salty.

■■ GRAVY BROWNER ■■

WHAT TO USE INSTEAD

Strong black coffee.   To darken and deepen the flavor of gravy made from pan drippings, add the coffee, half a teaspoon at a time. Taste the gravy as you add the coffee; your aim is to enrich flavor and color without making the gravy taste like coffee.

Saffron.   To make a chicken soup or chicken sauce deep yellow without using chicken fat or egg yolks, add a pinch of saffron—but only a pinch. Saffron's flavor is very intense.

■■ HERBAL VINEGARS ■■

WHAT TO USE INSTEAD

Distilled white vinegar plus fresh or dried herbs.   Steep ¼ teaspoon dried tarragon or sage or a sprig of fresh tarragon in a bottle of vinegar for at least forty-eight hours, then use the vinegar in salad dressings. Or simply add a pinch of herbs to your regular vinegar-and-oil dressing.

■■   HOT PEPPER SAUCE   ■■

WHAT TO USE INSTEAD

Cayenne pepper.   One quarter teaspoon whole cayenne pepper seeds or ⅛ teaspoon ground cayenne pepper = 3 to 4 drops hot pepper sauce. (All "hot pepper" sauces are made from hot capsicum peppers; tabasco sauce is a hot pepper sauce made from a capsicum variety known as tabasco.)

■■   MEAT TENDERIZER   ■■

WHAT TO USE INSTEAD

Beer, wine, vinegar and sugar (for "sweet and sour"), or yogurt.   Each of these acid marinades will break down proteins on the surface of the meat, making the meat more tender.

A meat mallet.   This tenderizes the old-fashioned way, by mechanically breaking down muscle fibers as you pound the meat.

■   NON-STICK   ■
■   COOKING SPRAY   ■

WHAT TO USE INSTEAD

Corn oil.   When you check the label on a can of "nonstick spray," you'll find that what you're actually spraying onto your frying pan is vegetable oil plus a propellant to get the oil out of the can. As an economical alternative, you can apply a thin film of corn oil to the pan, then wipe it off with a paper towel. The thin film that's left should work just as well as the more expensive spray.

PARCHMENT BAKING PAPER

WHAT TO USE INSTEAD

Waxed paper or aluminum foil.   Parchment baking paper is a silicone-coated paper used to line a baking pan or to make an envelope in which to steam fish *en papillote.* You can use waxed paper as a substitute to line a cake pan. If you butter the waxed paper, you can also use it to line a pan when baking bread (bread dough sticks to unbuttered waxed paper). Either waxed paper or aluminum foil will keep a meat loaf from sticking to a baking pan. Waxed paper crumples when it gets wet, so you can't use it as a substitute when steaming fish; for that you need an envelope of aluminum foil.

PREPARED MUSTARD

WHAT TO USE INSTEAD

Dry mustard.   In cooking, substitute 1 teaspoon dry mustard for each tablespoon of prepared mustard in a sauce, marinade, or salad dressing.

SEA SALT

WHAT TO USE INSTEAD

Table salt.   All salt, whether extracted from sea water (sea salt) or taken from the earth (table salt), is the same chemical combination of sodium and chloride ions. Some table salt contains added iodine which helps to protect you against goiter; all sea salt is naturally iodized.

■■ TAMARI ■■

WHAT TO USE INSTEAD

Soy sauce. Tamari, an ingredient in many Oriental recipes, is a soy sauce, a sauce made from fermented soybeans. Because it is fermented for a longer period of time than ordinary soy sauce, it has a stronger, richer taste. For all practical purposes, the two are interchangeable in cooking.

■■ TOMATO SAUCE ■■

WHAT TO USE INSTEAD

Tomato paste. One 6-ounce can of tomato paste plus one can water = 12 ounces (1 ½ cups) tomato sauce. To match the flavor of commercial tomato sauce, add salt and sugar to taste.

■■ VINEGAR ■■

WHAT TO USE INSTEAD

Lemon juice, dry vermouth, or dry white wine. Lemon juice diluted with water substitutes well for distilled white vinegar in salad dressings. The wines may be used in place of vinegar in marinades.

■■ WINE VINEGAR ■■

WHAT TO USE INSTEAD

Distilled white vinegar plus dry red wine. Mix 1 teaspoons wine with 2 tablespoons vinegar and use as recipe directs.

Leftover dry red wine. A bottle of wine that's been open a week or more may be perfect for your salad, if not your glass. Taste the dressing before serving; if the flavor is too strong, add water to dilute to taste.

NOTES: YOUR OWN ALTERNATIVES

_____

_____

_____

_____

_____

_____

_____

_____

_____

_____

_____

_____

_____

_____

_____

_____

_____

HERBS & SPICES

What's the difference
between an herb and a spice?
Spices are the seasonings
from tropical plants;
herbs, the seasonings from plants
that grow in temperate zones.
Generally,
a spice comes from a woody
plant, an herb from
a plant without wood.
These aromatic plant products
are a cook's delight,
especially when the cook
knows what to use
when what he or she wants to use
isn't at hand.

■■   ALLSPICE   ■■

WHAT TO USE INSTEAD

Equal parts ground cinnamon, cloves, and nutmeg. For
example, as a substitute for ¼ to ½ teaspoon allspice, combine ¼ teaspoon each cinnamon and cloves, plus ⅛ teaspoon
nutmeg; then measure out what you need.

■■   ANISE   ■■

WHAT TO USE INSTEAD

Ground fennel seed. Although the flavor of fennel is weak-
er and more delicate than that of anise, both taste distinctly
like licorice.

■■   BLACK PEPPER   ■■

WHAT TO USE INSTEAD

White pepper. Ground white pepper tastes exactly like
ground black pepper but it is more attractive in white sauces
or cream soups.

■■   BOUQUET GARNI   ■■

WHAT TO USE INSTEAD

Dry vermouth. It is not exactly the same, but when the alcohol in the vermouth evaporates during cooking what re-
mains is the pleasant taste of the herbs used to flavor the
wine.

■■   **CASSIA**   ■■

WHAT TO USE INSTEAD

Cinnamon.   Cassia and cinnamon are similar in taste, but cassia is much less expensive. That's why virtually all the "cinnamon" sold in this country is actually cassia.

■■   **CAYENNE PEPPER**   ■■

WHAT TO USE INSTEAD

Hot pepper sauce (such as Tabasco sauce).   Three to four drops hot pepper sauce = ⅛ teaspoon ground red pepper or ¼ teaspoon whole seeds.

■■   **CHERVIL**   ■■

WHAT TO USE INSTEAD

Parsley.   Its flavor is similar to chervil's, but stronger.

■■   **CHIVES**   ■■

WHAT TO USE INSTEAD

Snipped green tops of scallions.   The flavor is slightly stronger but a pretty good match in salads or on top of a baked potato.

■■   **CUMIN**   ■■

WHAT TO USE INSTEAD

Ground caraway seeds.   This one's a real surprise. The

flavor of the ground caraway seeds is similar to the flavor of cumin seeds, although lighter and more refined.

■■   FRESH HERBS AND SPICES   ■■

WHAT TO USE INSTEAD

Dried herbs and spices.   As a general rule, a teaspoon of dried herb or spice is equivalent to a tablespoon of fresh herb or spice.

■■   GARLIC   ■■

WHAT TO USE INSTEAD

Garlic powder, dried minced garlic, or garlic salt.   One-eighth teaspoon garlic powder, ⅛ teaspoon dried minced garlic, or 1 teaspoon garlic salt = one clove fresh garlic. If you choose the garlic salt as a substitute, be sure to taste the dish before adding salt.

■■   GINGER   ■■

WHAT TO USE INSTEAD

Ground, dried, or candied ginger.   One tablespoon of chopped candied ginger, washed to remove the sugar, or ⅛ teaspoon ground ginger = 1 tablespoon grated fresh ginger.

■■   HORSERADISH   ■■

WHAT TO USE INSTEAD

Prepared horseradish.   Two tablespoons bottled prepared

horseradish or 1 teaspoon dried grated horseradish = 1 tablespoon grated fresh horseradish.

■■   MACE   ■■

WHAT TO USE INSTEAD

Nutmeg.   Nutmeg is the kernel of the fruit of an evergreen tree native to Indonesia; mace is the membrane covering the kernel. Nutmeg and mace have the same basic flavor, but nutmeg's is more intense.

■■   MARJORAM   ■■

WHAT TO USE INSTEAD

Oregano.   Oregano is a wild marjoram. Its flavor is similar to marjoram's, but sharper and spicier.

■■   OREGANO   ■■

WHAT TO USE INSTEAD

Marjoram.   Marjoram's flavor is similar to that of oregano (a wild marjoram), but milder and less spicy.

Thyme.   Not as good a match as marjoram, but it will do if you're caught short.

■■   PICKLING SPICE   ■■

WHAT TO USE INSTEAD

A mixture of allspice, crumbled bay leaves, black or white pepper (whole or ground), cinnamon, whole cloves, corian-

der, ginger, and mustard seed. That's what you will find in commercial pickling spices. Put the spices in a small cheesecloth bag or teaball, and add it to your soup or stew. Then, remove the spices before you serve the dish.

■■ SAFFRON ■■

WHAT TO USE INSTEAD

Annatto. Annatto, which also colors food golden yellow, is a good substitute because it is much less expensive than saffron and doesn't have saffron's medicinal flavor.

Turmeric. When using turmeric in place of saffron, use just enough to make the food golden. If you use more, the dish may taste gingery and astringent.

■■ VANILLA BEAN ■■

WHAT TO USE INSTEAD

Vanilla extract. The flavor of 1 teaspoon vanilla extract equals the flavor of 1 inch scraped vanilla bean.

NOTES: YOUR OWN ALTERNATIVES

_____

_____

_____

_____

_____

_____

_____

_____

_____

_____

_____

_____

_____

_____

_____

_____

_____

_____

_____

_____

_____

_____

_____

_____

_____

_____

_____

_____

TABLE OF EQUIVALENT MEASUREMENTS

How many
teaspoons in a tablespoon?
How many tablespoons in a cup?
How many grams in an ounce?
How many liters in a quart?
Whether you're trying to
adapt a recipe,
substituting a liquid for a solid,
or simply wrestling
with the metric system,
the right answers
may spell the difference
between failure and success.
Here is a useful chart.

TABLE OF
EQUIVALENT MEASUREMENTS

MEASURING LIQUIDS

1 teaspoon	=	80 drops
		⅓ tablespoon
1 tablespoon	=	3 teaspoons
		½ fluid ounce
¼ cup	=	12 teaspoons
		4 tablespoons
		2 fluid ounces
½ cup	=	24 teaspoons
		8 tablespoons
		4 fluid ounces
		¼ pint
1 cup	=	48 teaspoons
		16 tablespoons
		8 fluid ounces
		½ pint
		¼ quart
		237 milliliters (250 ml = ¼ liter)
1 fluid ounce	=	6 teaspoons
		2 tablespoons
		30 milliliters
1 fluid pint	=	2 cups
		16 fluid ounces
		½ fluid quart
		474 milliliters (500 ml = ½ liter)
1 fluid quart	=	4 cups
		32 fluid ounces
		2 fluid pints
		¼ fluid gallon
		946 milliliters (0.946 liters)

1 liter	=	1,000 milliliters
		1.06 liquid quarts
		4.22 cups
		33.3 liquid ounces

MEASURING SOLIDS

1 ounce	=	28.35 grams
3.5 ounces	=	100 grams
16 ounces	=	1 pound
1 pound	=	454 grams

Source: *Nutritive Value of Foods*, Home and Garden Bulletin No. 72 (Washington, D.C.: USDA, 1985), National Bureau of Standards, Gaithersburg, Md.

SOURCES

GENERAL COOKBOOKS

Anderson, Jean and Hamna, Elaine, *The Doubleday Cookbook* (Garden City, New York: Doubleday & Company, 1975)

The Fanny Farmer Cookbook (Boston: Little Brown, 1965).

Coulson, Zoe, ed., *The Good New Housekeeping Cookbook* (New York: Hearst Books, 1986)

Rombauer, Irma S., and Becker, Marion Rombauer, *Joy of Cooking* (Indianapolis: Bobbs Merrill, 1984)

The Settlement Cookbook (New York: Simon and Schuster, 1976)

COOKBOOKS FOR SPECIAL DIETS

The American Heart Association Cookbook (New York: Ballantine Books, 1984).

Eisenberg, Arlene, Eisenberg, Heidi, Eisenberg, Sandee, *The Special Guest Cookbook* (New York: Beaufort Books, 1982)

Goodman, Harriet Wilensky, and Morse, Barbara, *Just What the Doctor Ordered* (New York: Holt, Rinehart and Winston, 1982)

Hamrick, Becky, and Weisenfeld, S.L., M.D., *The Egg-free, Milk-free, Wheat-free Cookbook* (New York: Harper & Row, 1981)

BOOKS ABOUT HERBS & SPICES

Lust, John, *The Herb Book* (New York: Bantam Books, 1983)

Rosengarten, Frederic Sr., *The Book of Spices* (New York: Jove, 1981)

Taylor's Guide to Vegetables and Herbs (Boston: Houghton Mifflin, 1987)

BOOKS ABOUT HEALTH & HEALTH PRODUCTS

Berkow, Robert, ed., *The Merck Manual,* 14th edition (Rahway, N.J.: Merck, Sharp & Dohme Research Laboratories, 1982)

The Boston Women's Health Book Collective, *The New Our Bodies, Ourselves* (New York: Simon & Schuster, 1984)

The Columbia University College of Physicians and Surgeons Complete Home Medical Guide (New York: Crown Publishers, 1985)

Conry, Tom, *Consumer's Guide to Cosmetics* (Garden City, New York: Anchor Books, 1980)

Graedon, Joe, *The People's Pharmacy* (New York: St. Martin's Press, 1976) and *The People's Pharmacy-2* (New York: Avon Books, 1980)

Krupp, Marcus A., Chatton Milton J., Tierney, Lawrence M., Jr., *Current Medical Diagnosis and Treatment 1986* (Los Altos, California: Lange Medical Publications, 1986)

The American Red Cross, *Standard First Aid & Personal Safety* (Garden City, New York: Doubleday & Company, 1973)

Spock, Benjamin, *Baby and Child Care* (New York: Pocket Books, 1976)

Zamm, Alfred V., and Gannon, Robert, *Why Your House May Endanger Your Health* (New York: Simon and Schuster, 1980)

Zimmerman, David R., *The Essential Guide to Nonprescription Drugs* (New York: Harper & Row, 1983)

BOOKS ABOUT FOOD CONTENT & CHEMISTRY

Grosser, Arthur, *The Cookbook Decoder* (New York: Warner Books, 1981)

McGee, Harold, *On Food and Cooking* (New York: Charles Scribner's Sons, 1984)

Nutritive Value of Foods, Home and Garden Bulletin No. 72 (Washington, D.C.: USDA, 1985)

COOKING TIPS & HOUSEHOLD HINTS

Arkin, Frieda, *Kitchen Wisdom* (New York: Holt, Rinehart & Winston, 1977)

Mager, N.H., and S.K., *The Household Encyclopedia* (New York: Pocket Books, 1975)

Moore, Alma Chestnut, *How to Clean Everything* (New York: Simon and Schuster, 1968)

Stagg, Camille, *The Cook's Advisor* (Brattleboro, Vt.: The Stephen Green Press, 1982)

Townsend, Doris, *The Cook's Companion* (New York: Crown Publishers, 1978)

ORGANIZATIONS

American Diabetes Association, 1660 Duke Street, Alexandria VA 22314 (800) 232-3472

The American Dietetic Association, 430 North Michigan Avenue, Chicago IL 60611 (301) 280-5091

American Heart Association, 7320 Greenville Avenue, Dallas TX 75231 (214) 750-5300

Arthritis Foundation, 1314 Spring Street N.W., Atlanta GA (404) 872-7100

INDEX